Jeff Mann
REBELS

Rebels
Copyright © 2015 Jeff Mann. All rights reserved. No part of this work may be reproduced or utilized in any form or by any means, electronic or mechanical, including photocopying, microfilm, and recording, or by any information storage and retrieval system, without permission in writing from the publisher.

Published in 2015 by Lethe Press, Inc.
118 Heritage Avenue • Maple Shade, NJ 08052-3018
www.lethepressbooks.com • lethepress@aol.com
ISBN-10: 1590211146
ISBN-13: 978-1590211144

Illustrations are copyright © their artists. Credits for original publications appear on page 166, which constitutes a continuation of this copyright page.

Set in Palatino and Landsdowne.
Front cover art and design: Elizabeth Leggett
Interior and back cover design: Anne Bean
Author photograph: L.S. King

Lethe Press
Maple Shade, NJ

In memory of my Confederate ancestor, Isaac Green Carden.

For my favorite Yankee, John Ross.

Many thanks to publisher Steve Berman, book designer Anne Bean, and the talented artists who've made this an especially handsome book.

Table Of Contents

List of Illustrations iv

I.
The Battle Of Scary Creek 3
Manassas Picnic 6
Cooking For Yankees 7
Cheat Summit Fort 8
Buckwheat Cakes 11
Graves, Camp Allegheny. 12
Driving To Washington, D.C. 16
In The Capital Of The Enemy 18

II.
Snow Quilt 23
A Brief Tour Of McDowell, Virginia 24
Two Woodstock Menus 26
Beast Butler 28
Ashby Fantasia 1 30
Confederate Kiss 32
Turner Ashby Monument, Chestnut Ridge 34
Horizontal Refreshments, 1862 36
Malvern Hill 39
The Shepherdstown Sweet Shop 42

Two Lovers At Antietam Battlefield 44
The Sweetest Music 46
Fredericksburg Battlefield 48

III.
The Gallant Pelham 53
Chancellorsville 55
Lemon 57
Weeping Freak 60
Cherry Picking 62
A Few Yards Of Pickett's Charge 64
The Fourth Of July 67
French Restaurant, Gettysburg 70

IV.
January Night, Johnson's Island 75
The Battle Of Cloyd's Farm 77
The Battle Of New River Bridge—Radford, Virginia 81
Sheetz In The Wilderness 83
Light Rain At Saunders Field 85
Lee To The Rear 88
The Sweet Studs Of Spotsylvania 92
Making Love To Stuart 95
Jeb Stuart In The Suburbs 98
Cherry Petals, VMI 100
Cold Harbor 104
A Roughed-Up Redneck 107
After The Reenactment 1 108
After The Reenactment 2 110
Sheridan Circle 112
Shep—December 1864 115
Shep—Prayer After The Great Snowball Battle 118

V.

Lexington Busboy	123
Escaping Chimborazo	124
The Death Of Beautiful Men	126
The Fall Of Richmond	129
Belle Isle Prison Camp	134
"Dixie"	139
Camp Chase	143
Grand Opening, Museum Of The Confederacy, Appomattox	146
Ashby Fantasia 2	151
The Rebs In Westview Cemetery	154
Laurel Hill	156
Confederate Gravestone, Charlotte Court House	160
Notes	163
Acknowledgments	166

List of Illustrations

The Battle of Scary Creek — Ben Baldwin 4
Buckwheat Cakes — Benedicte Caillat 10
Graves, Camp Allegheny — Rob Appleby 15
Snow Quilt — Nicholas Jackson 22
Confederate Kiss — Kirbi Fagan. 33
Horizontal Refreshments, 1862 — Orion Zangara 37
The Gallant Pelham — Craig LaRotonda 52
Lemon — Stephanie Ann Helgeson 58
A Few Yards of Pickett's Charge — Graham Corcoran. 65
January Night, Johnson's Island — Paulina Wyrt 74
Making Love to Stuart — Ashley Holt 96
Cherry Petals, VMI — Laura Hallett 102
Sheridan Circle — Galen Dara 113
Lexington Busboy — Jon Hunt 122
The Death of Beautiful Men — Tijmen Ploeger. 127
"Dixie" — Erin Maala. 141
Ashby Fantasia 2 — Jason Blower 152
Laurel Hill — Joanna Barnum 157
Cicada — Benedicte Caillat 161
Civil War Camp Sentry, Rappahannock Station, Virginia — Edwin Forbes. 166

I.

The Battle of Scary Creek

Your first battle, most likely, great-great-grandfather Carden,
holding this bridge over Scary Creek against the Yankees.

"First Confederate victory in Kanawha Valley fought here
July 17th, 1861," says the historical marker, set between

the creek's mouth and my favorite redneck restaurant
in all of West Virginia, the Red Line Diner, where for years,

in predatory fantasy abducting many a bearded and tattooed
country boy, unknowingly I have gobbled hot dogs and fries

on the very spot where your foes stood. In my childhood,
you were nothing more than a plaque in the family graveyard—

Isaac G. Carden West Virginia Pvt Lowry's Btry VA Lt Arty
Confederate States Army Aug 10 1841 Feb 28 1932—

but now, thanks to genealogical research, a handful of e-file
photographs, and one lime-green regimental history, I see you

clearly, there on the creek's far bank, frightened boy who could be
my fraternal twin, the same dark hair and eyes and beard I bore

at that age, a few weeks short of your twentieth birthday, as
you sweat through your gray jacket, curse the bluecoats, labor

beside your brothers John and Allen, wielding the rammer,
sponge, and worm, head ringing with the cannons' boom,

nose burning with the acrid smoke. Over dinner last week,
a friend mentioned research that suggests an ancestor's

traumas can be carried within the genes. If so, the Battle
of Scary Creek is threaded inside my cells, Isaac, which would explain

why today's part of me sits in the diner's air-conditioned cool,
enjoying hot dogs and iced tea, while someone deeper, older,

riven by kinship and history, helps load the gun, screams
hate against the invaders, wipes black bangs from his brow,

and clears weeds from about your grave plaque in the hilltop
cemetery where my less-than-valiant ashes will one day join yours.

Manassas Picnic

> It was after the beaten army had crossed Bull Run that the real trouble
> came, and the fault lies less with the soldiers than with the reckless
> Washington civilians who had supposed that the edge of a battlefield
> would be an ideal place for a picnic.
> —Bruce Catton, *The Civil War*

Rest here, Miss Letitia, in the shade of this linden.
Hettie, lay down the blanket first. No need
for ladies to stain their skirts. Down there's
the little creek they call Bull Run. Now,

let's see. Here's cheese. Roast chicken, soft rolls,
sour pickles, cold beef and mustard. Gingerbread,
and—oh, Hettie, well done!—Lady Baltimore cake.
Just a thimbleful of wine? A toast then. To Lincoln!

And McDowell! Look at our grand blue lines.
How the flags unfurl in Virginia wind, our blessed
red, white and blue. Black smoke now, see?

The first sharp volley of muskets. That roar—they've let
the cannon loose. Here's to the rebellion's so-swift
end. Drink up. We'll have beat them in a day.

Cooking For Yankees

Here's tonight's hillbilly host, mine own Daddy Bear self,
bushy salt-and-pepper beard of a middle-aged mountain man,

older by a decade than Stonewall Jackson when he died.
Here's my husbear John, descendant of William Bradford, pure

Yankee stock: mother from Taunton, father from Worchester.
Here are our guests, my favorite colleagues: Mannahatta

Joe, Boston Charlene, and her son Nick, 13, same age as
Confederate boy-soldier John Sloan, who lost a leg

at Farmington and grieved his loss by claiming, "I have
but one regret I shall not soon be able to get at the enemy."

My Yankees batten down, a Southern feast of country ham,
sweet-glazed, with potato salad, broccoli salad, deviled eggs.

I count the years since '64, when Hunter and Sheridan,
those Federal fuckers, burnt the houses, blackened the Valley,

left us Rebs to starve. 144 summers decayed
since Appomattox, shame I chew still, piling the guns

in April grass. Had I met these faces in the smoke
and screech of shell, I would have fought till someone

bled and fell. Instead I fill glasses with tawny port,
help Mizz Charlene whip cream fog-thick for Scottish trifle.

Cheat Summit Fort

Little's left
of your Yankee walls—once
fourteen feet high and eight feet
thick, so claims the marker.
God help you, the first snows
on Cheat Mountain's heights
came in August that year.
Sweet foes, within your parapets
you were snugged like grubs
immured for the winter,
dying just as fast as my forebears
atop Allegheny Mountain, in
the Rebel camp across the valley.
Gasping and hacking, flux-
hunched in latrine ditches,
did you pine and sob for
the flatlands of Indiana
you'd left behind all for
the grand idea of Union?
Did the sough of wind in spruce
at four thousand feet remind
you of the way summer
rippled the long rows of corn
back home? I walk the great circle
of your earthworks, nothing now
but a low concentric wave
humping soil, henge once of
a red deity moving blue pawns
against gray. Sharp and wintry
drizzle, even on the first of May,

but the ferns, fragile as gold-
green lace, are unfurling, flags
of another country, one as yet
unconquered. There's a fire pit
here, to match those you shivered
around, a few Bud Light bottles
tossed down. The luckier boys
moved on come spring's relief,
that April of 1862. The weaker,
never again to see Indiana,
remained atop the foreign
mountaintop, inside graves
over which I am ready to tip
my STARS AND BARS FOREVER
cap to honor a valiant enemy, but
no, "the fort cemetery was destroyed
by strip mining while the site
was in private ownership,"
says the marker. I can see it
so clearly, the sad bones exhumed
like doggie treats, buried hastily
elsewhere. You began as patriots,
ended as invalids, and, after that,
as mere inconvenience, something
unpleasant that needed shifting,
macabre delay between the finding
and the eager claiming of coal.

Buckwheat Cakes

I have four-wheeled where they walked,
the summer heights of Highland County,
but I will never know ecstasy approaching that
which Rebel soldiers fell into after trudging
fifteen miles in snow. Isaac Coles,
one of six, long remembered *the comfort,
warmth and fragrance of that tidy, genial
most marvelous kitchen…like a dream,
too much like fiction in those hard days,
to feel it could be true*, the ways
*pans shone like mirrors,…crockery
glistened.* They sat, cold, starved,
exhausted, watching her cook,
a Mrs. Beveridge, as she *stood by
the stove frying buckwheat cakes for
her country's hungry soldiers.* She was
Hebe bearing ambrosia, that portly
farm wife near Monterey, pouring out
real mountain maple syrup one may
buy in Highland County yet. After dinner,
upstairs and into feather beds they went,
these boys used by now to shelter tents,
the stink of wet wool, fitful sleep in
rolls of oilcloth. I stand beside the bed
and watch them snore; I brush crumbs
from their syrup-sticky lips. This is
the sweetest sleep a man will ever
know or need. This is an enviable
      eternity.

Graves, Camp Allegheny

1.
I've been here many times without finding them,
having kept to the public side of barbed wire, as
historical markers demand, staying off private land.
The Angel of History, I call him—a middle-aged local
sitting in his pickup at this isolate spot, this windswept
mountaintop, as if he were waiting for us, who steps out
as we two drive up and offers to show us around, who turns
out to be a godsent expert on the battle and the camp—
he is not so timid, showing the way between strands
of said barbed wire, leading us to two sets of graves.

2.
They have planted a red spruce forest
around you back in the 1960's, scaly trunks
equally spaced, rising straight as rows
of temple columns around your graves.
You have lain here since the 1860's,
victims most likely of disease, the war's
first bitter winter, when horses froze
standing up and epidemics swept the camp.
No doubt you had markers once,
wooden ones made by comrades who
survived you, but those have vanished,
and now the only indications that
your bones rest here, a few feet
beneath the needle-carpeted forest floor,
are these four sunken indentations,
man-length, such as a potter's thumb

might make in clay. Into the shallow dips
the wind blows leaves, and so the leaves
collect. Perhaps those fates who felled you
have after all decided that you deserve
an extra blanket, and a few spring beauties
as mourning bouquets, blossoming from
mountain earth you joined long ago.

3.
Only the base of the obelisk remains.
This high, four thousand feet atop
Allegheny Mountain, the sarvis
blooms still, pinwheels of snow,
as if deliberately planted
to mark the head of your graves.
Such small stones, barely calf-high,
like those of infants, the stillborn.
Names long worn off. You were here,
living long enough to become men
but little longer, these memorials proof
you were more than numbers in fact-heavy
history books. Were I less proper, wilder,
I would sit cross-legged above you, drink
a goodly bit of bourbon and pour
the rest into the ground, as if to regale
the thirsty dead. You loved home, yet
you chose to ascend this awful height.
You knew misery more than most,
and then you died. Suffering's
only reward is remembrance.
I gladly give you that. I envy you
this quiet bed at pasture's edge,
beneath the drifting sarvis. I envy
you your high, windswept home.

4.
The Angel points out heaps of rubble that once
were barracks chimneys, shakes our hands, climbs into
his truck, and heads down the dirt road that used
to be the Staunton/Parkersburg Turnpike. Sweet
Yankee husband, how tolerant you are, following me
from Rebel site to Rebel site without a chiding word. Time
to leave the war, descend the mountain, re-enter spring,
leave the dead behind. For such patience, I promise you
Southern delights: pulled pork barbeque at Smiley's
truck stop, with cole slaw and sweet iced tea. How lucky
we are still to bear the burden of appetite. How lucky
we are inside this era, blessed by the ordinary, far
from the shriek of shell, the smoky curse of valor.

Driving to Washington, D.C.

Past Salem, where Jubal Early's men
burnt caissons, captured horses,
drove fleeing Yankees west into the mountains.

Past Lexington, where's Stonewall's buried,
where Hunter burnt VMI, where Lee sleeps
in marble within his brick-and-ivy chapel.

Past Staunton, where girls at the Virginia Female Institute
hid hams from invading bluecoats, where J.E.B. Stuart's
widow served as principal for nineteen years.

Past Harrisonburg, the condo-swallowed
monument marking where black-bearded Turner Ashby fell,
unhorsed, shot through the heart.

Stopping for barbeque in Elkton—good pulled pork,
cole slaw, and someone's shrill piping child,
wondering how parents tolerate that prattle.

Past a hot shirtless hitchhiker John wants
to pick up—what coward in me insists
we not? The same craven that has limited Eros all my life.

Up over Swift Run Gap, where Henry Kyd Douglas
galloped one *impenetrable stormy night*,
carrying crucial information from Jackson to Ewell.

Past Brandy Station,
where Stuart's cavalry paraded, where
they smashed into Federals and clashed for twelve hours.

Past Kelly's Ford, where the Gallant Pelham died,
his body plucked from the enemy like that
of Patroclus, and *Stuart wept aloud over the body of his young hero.*

Past Manassas, where Bee shouted,
"Look, there is Jackson with his Virginians, standing
like a stone wall!" and so into the capital of the enemy.

In the Capital of the Enemy

Where the bluecoats once swirled, the prostitutes festered,
whoredom became Federal Triangle. Where Sherman savored

his Grand March of victory, where Grant smoked himself
closer to throat cancer. Where Lincoln imprisoned

the Copperheads without due process or trial, signed
his Proclamation, breathed his last. This city's nothing

to a gray-beard hedonist like me but restaurants and bars.
I recommend the calamari at Raku, the grilled octopus

at Jaleo. I recommend the Green Lantern on Thursdays—
good video porn, plus shirtless boys drink free. There's

the D.C. Eagle for leather, the Motley Bar for Bear Happy Hour,
the Leather Rack for slave collars and Wiffle-ball gags.

(Aren't we Rebs supposed to be overheated and wild?
Intemperate, violent, drunken, coarse, etc.?)

Finally, I recommend an iPhone and Grindr, for then,
in between perusals of *Wearing of the Gray*, one can

indulge in profounder urban pleasures. For instance,
this submissive Yankee with gym-fit body and graying goatee

who visits our hotel room just long enough to suck off,
efficiently, speedily, and with lip-smacking fervor,

this visiting Southerner and his partner. Soon enough
our stranger's off to the gym, never to be seen again,

and we're swilling margaritas and snarfing burritos
at Lauriol Plaza, drinking a toast to Northern hospitality.

Snow Quilt

He is sleeping in a field between
Berkeley Springs and Hancock,
he and his Rebs exhausted from
the march. After midnight a wet
finger brushes his brow, and he
murmurs awake, pulls the damp
blanket over his face and sleeps
again, corpse-still. When
he wakes in first light, he wakes
warm, too warm, tosses off
his blanket, scatters five inches of
mountain snow that sheltered him
in the night like a crystal shield of
righteousness, like a father's arms,
and he looks about him at
the *great logs of men…covered over
with snow and as quiet as graves*,
rising one by one warm, amazed,
shaking off God's wool—and oh,
how they wish they might weave
of snow durable and lasting
blankets, as snow shields tender
wheat and the earth-tamped hope
of seeds—till one man breaks the mood,
shouting, "Great Jehosophat!
The Resurrection!" and they
are up, starting small fires for
a spitted beef and hardtack breakfast.

A Brief Tour of McDowell, Virginia

> God blessed our arms with victory at McDowell yesterday.
> —Stonewall Jackson

One by one, they pass. Stonewall's men
on Sitlington's Hill, in the new gold-green
leaves of May and the sharp stink of powder,
artillery's thunderclap, the splintered Yanks
retreating west. In the church, men in blue,
later men in gray, choking up blood, sobbing,
carving dates and initials in brick, then limping
on, if they can; remaining, if they cannot,
in the grassy graveyard across the road. Next,
the Maple Syrup Festival: crowded pancake
breakfasts, churchgoers and breeders,
the ever-fertile Southern devout, snapping
up sausage and excoriating sin. And now,
two modern mountain men, a warm day
four-wheeling through Highland County,
in the sweetest fucking Toyota Tacoma
ever built. Red goatee and black goatee,
cowboy boots and dusters, cowboy hats,
they're striding through the biannual
Battlefield Days, May breeze beard-soft
and scuffing dust from the road. They're
praising Jackson, patting gravestones, buying
syrup in a country store. They're sitting on
the truck's tailgate, sipping iced tea, gobbling
rat cheese and chicken salad sandwiches.

Soon, they'll drive deeper, down back roads,
into secret, a family cabin, a mountain cove,
the furtive exile their mingled bodies make.
Beside a trickling lick, one will kneel, suck
his buddy's cock, kiss and lick his buddy's
boots. One will strip the other, rope him
to a gleaming green-gold willow, gag him
tight, beat him with a belt. But for now
both men are all they seem, happy sons
of the South, filling simple hungers
where glorious forebears once kicked
invaders' ass. For now, the sun is theirs,
the land is home, they belong entirely.

Two Woodstock Menus

In McDonald's, it is autumn 1991. I'm in love,
but Thomas and his husband have just moved
north, have vanished like sunlit peach petal,
windowpane frost, the mica-glitter hopes

of youth, and I am having lunch—coffee,
an unmemorable burger—with Buck,
the fay roommate they left behind,
who knows nothing of how I ache,

who—useless irony—wants me as I
do not want him. We have broken up
a drive to D.C. with this brief stop
at Woodstock, and, see, I smile and chat

as if I were still whole, as if my guts
were not untangled, strung like soldiers'
across dock and bloody stubble, as if
my body were not one hairy, lonely lie,

for from that lost lover and that long
adultery I have learned to betray
with the best, and so, embedded in
myself, I do not see, in a field nearby,

where it is early June and midnight, 1862,
my Rebs feasting on stores they seized
from fleeing Yanks. They are ravenous,
the foe might be on them tomorrow,

they have everything to lose,

and so they are *determined to place
a great portion of these viands beyond
the possibility of recapture.* It's a motley
menu, to be sure: *cake and pickled lobsters,*

*cheese, canned peaches, piccolomini
and candy, coffee, ale, and condensed milk.*
Eat up, boys, eat all you can. God knows
I did, gobbling cock-feast and armpit bush,

hairy buttocks, fur-nestled nipples, knowing
the enemy would soon arrive to rout me,
sensing what I stole would be surely stolen back.
This fate's what makes us kin: to feast, to savor

the last bite of lobster, the last bearded kiss,
and then to slowly starve. We leave Woodstock
now, you to march south, I to drive north. Different
centuries, but our futures converge. Soon we'll meet

on the same road, where empty haversacks are
dropped in mud, where youth's strength and soles
give out, where we are all brothers trudging bare
and bootless, leaving bloody footprints in the snow.

Beast Butler

> Benjamin Franklin Butler, military governor of New Orleans in 1862,
> is remembered by Southerners as "Beast Butler."
> —Thomas P. Lowry, M.D., *The Story the Soldiers Wouldn't Tell: Sex in the Civil War*

You were invaders. What did you expect
from the women of New Orleans? Petits fours?
Pain au chocolat? Creole ladies serve me these
and more, here on the Royal Sonesta's
concierge floor: martinis, fried crayfish,
goat cheese, creamy shrimp with pasta,
crab rangoon. I enjoy hospitality, not hate.
I am a citizen of this nation, not its foe,
and I was taught how to treat a lady. You, well…
obese and ill-favored troll, oleaginous, occupying
the conquered Crescent City, you received
a far less fattening, far more colorful welcome.
On a balcony like this one, where I sip cooling gin
far above the French Quarter, the ladies
pirouetted, raised their skirts, gave you a glimpse
of their nether parts. And your guest,
poor Farragut, upon his glorious head
they poured their chamber pots, in the face
of your soldiers spat their contempt. And so,
clever Beast, knowing how much Southern women
prize reputation, you passed Order No. 28:
it is ordered that hereafter, when any female
shall, by word, gesture or movement, insult
or show contempt for any officer or soldier
of the United States, she shall be regarded
and held liable to be treated as a woman
of the town, plying her avocation. And so

their detestation became a private thing.
Your name lingers, Beast, and the hate that still
engenders, and truth be told, the photos
remaining favor a lazing warthog, but I admit
I am biased in this regard. I only remember
that ceramic chamber pot behind glass, oh
rare relic, in the Museum of the Confederacy,
a thing of gleaming white, and, there, inside,
painted upon the pristine bottom, your face
with its surly brow, full jowls, mustachioed.
Ahh, the ladies lifted their skirts behind
the drapes and shutters that shielded them from
law and public light and so they relieved themselves,
covering your likeness with patriotic bladders
and bowels, and so I might do the same, given
a precious replica, yes, after two martinis
and in the name of those New Orleans ladies,
here's commemoration, Beast, ah, now, ahhh…

Ashby Fantasia 1

To my long list of sexual peculiarities,
I must now add eroticizing the dead. Not
necrophilia, that would be nasty, true, but
wishing for some way to suture time so as
to ravish those many hirsute heroes long lost,
never met. Rump-ranger romantic, reading
this online description of Rebel cavalry general
Turner Ashby, I fall desperately in love:

Dressed now in Confederate gray,
with gilt lace on his sleeves and collar, wearing
high top-boots with spurs and a broad-brimmed
black felt hat with a long black feather streaming
behind, his appearance was striking and attractive.
He stood about five feet eight inches in height and
probably weighed from 150 to 160 pounds… He was
muscular and wiry, rather thin than robust or rugged.
His hair and beard were as black as a raven's wing;
his eyes were soft and mahogany brown; a long,
sweeping mustache concealed his mouth, and a heavy
and long beard completely covered his breast.
His complexion was dark in keeping with
his other colorings. Altogether, he resembled
the pictures. . . of the early Crusaders.

Turner Ashby, muscle-cub,
I'll meet you anywhere. By the flower-hemmed
monument on Chestnut Ridge, where you yelled,
"Forward, my brave men!" then fell, shot through
the heart, dying in the arms of a boy who loved you.

By your grand grave in Winchester; by Rose Land
in Fauquier County, where you grew up. In
the leather bars of San Francisco, New York, D.C.
In my basement dungeon or the nearest BBQ joint.
Return. Take on your former dense and furry form.
Be my boy, my bottom, my house-slave in jockstrap,
dog collar, work boots. Crusader, you've suffered
long, suffered enough. Call me father, call me
savior. Let me sweep you onto my saddle-horn,
lift you into my arms, carry you far from death.

Confederate Kiss

Down by the broadening James, twilight
chants, thick with August. Along corridors
of crepe myrtle, boot heels are curving
        toward the graveyard,

Confederate captain and sergeant meeting
among headstones, on furtive leave, in dusk.
Birds roost noisily in the great trees,

as we unbutton gray, in a chest-clink
of meeting medals, the drawl of love-words,
bearded kisses rough with bourbon and tobacco.

So the sourwood's bells peal open
to bee-probe and nestle, the honeydew
splits juicily beneath the knife.
The oyster, prized, spills its liquor,
rosy champagne escapes its cork.
So the long-reformed addict takes
his first guilty, euphoric moonshine sip,
petals leap past potential into advantage.

Far from the fires of approving hearth
or stoic bivouac, our tongues' déjà vu,
our night-blooming surrenders.
The crepe myrtle's a brush of benediction, as

we cross swords, callused hands sliding through
moist nights of chest hair, fresh nakedness
lending purpose to Tidewater heat,
semen shuddering across vinca-dark grave sod.

Turner Ashby Monument, Chestnut Ridge

> General Ashby was a man of striking personal appearance, about five feet ten inches tall, with a well-proportioned figure, graceful and compact, black eyes, black hair, and a flowing black beard…Riding his black stallion, he looked like a knight of the olden time…
> —Henry Kyd Douglas, *I Rode With Stonewall*

Turner, you're hard to find, nineteenth-century
hero lost in the twenty-first-century sprawl
of Harrisonburg, Virginia. We're using
my husbear's fancy iPhone to track you,
past McDonald's and malls, aluminum-siding
housing muddle, one contemporary
abortion after another. The Daughters
have managed to save a few woods yet;
the spot where you died, bullet through
your Fauquier heart, is shaded still with
thick green oak-shade, though Chestnut
Ridge has nary a chestnut left, all brought
low by a foreign blight. There's nothing
left of you here either, save this photo on
the Civil War Trails marker. I touch
your face—onyx eyes, combed black
hair, full lips shaped for loving, the wild
dark bush of your beard. See, Turner,
more souls than I remember you. Bouquets
flank the rough stone memorial marking
where you soaked Valley earth with blood—
peony petals, areola-pink, browning along
the edges, the bright blue lupines' droop.
The Daughters, determined, indefatigable,
presiding goddesses, protectors of this grove,
horticulturalists of partisan memory, have

planted here and there hellebores, hostas,
the crimson emblems of bleeding heart.
You gasped your last in the arms of a boy
who loved you *as only a fearless young soldier*
can love his hero, and whose love was fully rewarded
by your love for him, a boy who's buried
near you now in Winchester. I am too far
away to offer any warmth or comfort, but
I hope he was handsome, hope he held you
close in your damp tent those bitter winter nights,
shared with you sips of whiskey, sparse rations,
hope he gave your famous melancholy a smile,
though the wishing, like the poem, is far less about
you than me. I pluck and pocket your bleeding
heart, the sort of satiny souvenir we lovers
of knights are addicted to, lovers of bravery
and beauty who never managed to live
those things ourselves, and now John's
iPhone has found a likely lunch, and we're off
through another gauntlet of shopping malls
to Panera, though we must sadly abjure bread.
Low-carbing, we'll settle for Cobb salads instead.

Horizontal Refreshments, 1862

*A few weeks before the Seven Days' campaign
a newspaper reported a large influx
of prostitutes of both sexes into the capital,
and remarked that "they have been disporting
themselves extensively on the sidewalks,
and in hacks and open carriages…
[indulging in] smirks and smiles, winks and…
remarks not of a choice kind in a loud voice,"*
says Bell Irvin Wiley in *The Life of Johnny Reb.*

◆

Thighs spread, he's sitting on the steps
of George Washington's equestrian monument
and chewing on a twig when I enter Capitol Square.
Black hair falling over his brow, unkempt beard
just as black, and eyes the color of the heavens
this Virginia June, he's the finest-looking little lad
I've glimpsed since the war began. Shirt open
in the heat, his breast is broad and hairy, his belly
famine-flat. I con him long enough to know
my rare luck, how the hirsute coquette poses,
winks, and flexes when other men stride by.

"One of our country's grand defenders!
On leave, sir?" he says upon my approach,
with a squeeze of his groin and a welcoming grin.
His scent's strong—hayfields and beast-musk,
sweat of a foam-bit stallion after being ridden long.
"A warm leave indeed. One provoking thirst.

Show me the nearest tavern, and I promise
a reward both liquid and abundant," that's all
it takes, along with a show of bills. In an hour,
God's blessing or not, I'll help his tight stagger
up the stairs to my rented room, pay whatever
sum required to strip him down, hold hard
his youth for hours, spend in first his mouth
and then his rump. His mercenary comfort

I'll clasp till dawn, till day demands my return
to the front. The memory of such delight,
albeit bought, will be a prize to clutch in the face
of the foe's advance, a treasure to cherish till the day
I fall—beneath fate's whimsy, ashen decrepitudes
of age, or an accursed smother of Union blue.

Malvern Hill

> *Wag the world how it will,*
> *Leaves must be green in Spring.*
> —Herman Melville, "Malvern Hill"

There is no hill that I can see,
        only this broad field, October brown,
                the gentlest of slopes, with Yankee

cannon poised and soundless
        at the crest. Lee tried to crush
                them here, sledgehammer swung

at a rattlesnake's pitted head,
        tried and failed, to my regret.
                What heights there were

the bluecoats had, the bluecoats
        kept, lines and lines
                of artillery blasting Confederate

troops, Union warships lobbing
        hot hells of shell from the nearby James.
                By the chimneyed ruins of the parsonage,

in the Honda my history-
        wearied husband naps, while I trudge,
                new work boots pinching, dyspeptic

after the wrong Richmond restaurant,
        up this silent slope, past the Rebel
                lines, past infantry's farthest gray

advance, across the dry-grass deadly
    open where 5,000 Southerners fell—
        where tiny balls of whizzing lead pierced

brain and lung, sliced hunger-sunk
    belly, shattered rib and breast-
        bone—at last achieving those Union guns,

warily patting a cannon wheel.
    So July night descended,
        smoking muzzles slowly cooled,

while *the rain began to fall*
    on the cruel scene and beat out
        the torches of brave fellows hunting

their wounded companions
    in the dark, in the howling
        of the storm, the cry of

the wounded and groans of
    the dying, the glare of the torch
        upon the faces of the dead

or into the shining eyes
    of the speechless wounded, looking up
        in hope of relief, the ground slippery

with a mixture of mud and blood,
    all in the dark, hopeless, starless night...
        Did you boys ever conceive, in your fighting

and in your dying,
    our coming centuries, belated
        spectators wandering preserved parks,

awed, curious, bored with peace?
> Could you picture prosperity-plump
>> descendants like I myself, sighing

with pride and sorrow, hiking trails
> where once your corpses heaped?
>> Defenders, invaders, all have vanished.

Only seasons conquer.
> Near the Union cannon, ripe fields
>> of soybeans yellow. I bend to stroke

the leaves, the fuzzy pods,
> to cup up the rich black dirt,
>> mingling root and seed and buried bullets.

The Shepherdstown Sweet Shop

for Eddy Pendarvis

Moulder Hall—One of many buildings in down town Shepherdstown that were used as hospitals when casualties *"filled every building and overflowed into the country round..."* Moulder Hall was used for amputations. Currently the building is used as a bakery and restaurant.
—*The Historical Marker Database*

It is, without question, the most profoundly
delicious Bavarian-cream-filled doughnut
I have ever greedily, lipsmackingly devoured.

The sheer weight of it's a marvel, heavy with
that heart luxuriant of sugar, egg, milk, vanilla.
I lap chocolate, tongue-probe cream, chew and sigh,

roll my eyes with rapture, while Antietam's wounded
are gasping all around me, upstairs and down.
My Rebels thrash and sob and bleed beneath

the Shepherdstown Sweet Shop's coffee bar,
beneath éclairs, bear claws, cookies, cupcakes,
beneath my feet. The doctor pulls out his bone saw,

his tourniquet. This black-bearded soldier's only
eighteen, from the same Virginia mountains as I,
his thigh shattered by grapeshot. Chloroform's

run out in the great battle's aftermath, so I rock him
in my arms, tip whiskey to his lips. He gulps and gulps
and smiles; he grips my hand, grits a stick I slip

between his teeth. I wipe black powder from his face,
squeeze his shoulder, smooth his sweaty hair. When he nods,
I help three others hold him down so the doctor may begin.

Two Lovers at Antietam Battlefield

I have carried this grudge for decades,
since fifth-grade history, first hearing
secession, Fort Sumter, General Lee,
Stonewall, President Davis, Appomattox.
Enthused with partisan zeal, my classmates
and I adopted nicknames among the Rebel
generals. I was Beauregard. Needless to say,
no Summers County boys—raised there
among the Southern mountains, where
the Confederate monument, in eternal
verdigris vigilance, looms by the courthouse—
would ever side with Yanks.

        Defeated.
Defeated. Who can forget or forgive that?
Yet here I am, standing inside Dunker Church,
strolling down Bloody Lane, with you, golden
boy, Billy Yank, son of Massachusetts.
Direct descendant of Pilgrims, father from
Shrewsbury, mother from Taunton. (Exotic
New England, home of the erstwhile enemy,
home now of lobster rolls, blueberry pie,
streets where we might be somewhat safer
holding hands than in my beloved South,
foreign lands where we even might be married.)
Today we walk

    this *veritable field of blood,*
where shy horses skirt corpse-heaps, the maimed
wriggle over earth like worms after hard rain,

night falls over cries for water and darkness
makes blue and gray indistinguishable.
A few paltry generations back, we might
have met in this field in a different, darker
manner, your Minié ball in my throat,
my Bowie knife in your gut, our limbs
intertwined in blood and mud. Instead,
I watch the rich way August light
glints your forearm hair to gold while
you indulge my eccentric and historic grief,
following my hours about the battlefield. Today
I lay down that grudge a bit, that heavy
haversack, to mourn them all, invader
and defender, Massachusetts and Virginia,
the green-sheen water under Burnside's
Bridge. With the sun, we retreat west,
as Lee's troops did, fording the Potomac,

back to Shepherdstown and the Sweet Shop's
marzipan-jeweled stollen, the Bavarian Inn's
gravy-topped spätzle and schnitzel. Lie close
tonight, husbear, Billy Yank, as who knows
how many furtive bluecoats and butternuts
did, despite piety and the supposed laws
of nature, in forest, tent, or smoky bivouac,
mingling beards and tongues and body hair,
blending patriotic saps, making another union,
another America.

The Sweetest Music

It is long gone, and no one living
has heard it. There were no
tape recorders at Manassas,
Fredericksburg, Chancellorsville,
to save the fabled Rebel Yell.
A merged *Whooo-Whoo-eee*,
say some scholars. Influenced
by rural-dwellers' hallooing,
fox-hunters' cries, say others.
If, according to scientists, sound
never ends, simply disperses,
it echoes, too minutely to hear,
in these hills yet, rough kin to
the *Yee-Haws* I raise, driving
back roads alone, when seized,
ever so rarely these midlife days,
by rapture. Kin to the wildcat's
scream my grandmother heard in
her mountainous youth, kin to
the keer of the hawk, balloo of
the hound, howl of the charging
Highlander, all that is fierce
and wild, a man atop a man,
thrusting, pounding, cresting,
gasping, *the sweetest music
I ever heard*, said Stonewall,
when, at Bunker Hill, after
prayers around the fire and
the evening tattoo, one man
raised it, and then another,

and then another, till the shout
sparked like fire from brigade
and division, from camp to
camp, and Jackson leant upon
a fence-rail in the autumn
moonlight listening to it climb
and roar and throb and fade,
the passing music of defiance.

Fredericksburg Battlefield

for Jane Varley

The night before the battlefield, our bivouac's
the campus guesthouse. Too much burgundy,
a few poems, a little piano. No soldier's
sick clutch beneath the breastbone this morning.

Hungover sinuses are my only discomfort,
and the regret a four-poster unused by love
engenders. I have not slept on the earth in years.

Despite all my petty rages, the only blood
I've ever drawn has been my own.
On this slaughtering ground shriveled
into park, we watch a movie, stare at still-life

exhibits, among the other tourists or pilgrims
or scholars. Sad to feel so little, so safe,
dull and detached. What is history

but a few copied pages of Catton
in my gray backpack? From the visitor's
center we wander out, beneath
the sifting topaz of willow oaks,

down orderly paths, past numbered
relics on the walking tour, past blinding
yellows of Norway maple seized by sun.

Behind this pocked stone wall,
I stand where the defenders stood.

I want to think two lovers or brothers were here,
watching that blue surf smash the breakwater,

then roll back repelled, beaching husks in its wake.
Gray as morning mist my Rebels gasp,
side by side in the Sunken Road, gray

as winter sky. This is how heroism sparks,
how it flames like gun barrels, Norway maples
in November. One man steadies the other's
elbow like honor, calming the other's fear,

defending the land as if it were kin.
Survival is one gift they pray for, their mutter
inaudible beneath gunfire and frosted beards.

That, or the grace of falling together,
as maple seeds unspool, fused shoulder to shoulder,
a helix of wings. From twig-ends they break loose
above bloodless stone, slip slanting along a modern breeze.

The Gallant Pelham

> Stuart wept aloud over the body of his young hero—his fidus Achates.
> —Henry Kyd Douglas, *I Rode with Stonewall*

John Pelham, Jeb Stuart's artillery pet,
fidus Achates they called him,
after Aeneas's faithful companion,
but this scene is older by far
than Rome, Latium, or Troy.
The boy has held back the Yanks
at Sharpsburg, an Alabama David
launching from his slingshot
stone after hissing stone, the boy
has broken the Feds at Fredericksburg,
damming up the blue waves, dancing
nimbly beneath their answering arcs
of cannon fire, Lee has dubbed him
the gallant Pelham, Stonewall has said,
*With a Pelham on each flank
I believe I could whip the world*, and now

like Patroclus, his body is swept
from the enemy's grasp, and now
Stuart bends over him, red beard
wet with winter and with grief,
cavalier fox tail brushing tenderly,
belatedly, the boy's beloved face, while
March snow melts on what warmth
is left in Pelham's cooling skin.
*Press forward, press forward to
glory and victory*, he shouted from

the saddle, before a flying fragment
of Federal shell shattered his head
like milkweed pod or walnut hull.
Only twenty-one years old. Stuart
cradles him, rocks him, and sobs.

Nested inside the scene, a god
does the same to a discus-maimed
beauty slowly fading into purple flower,
and a hero does the same to a hairy
wild man born of Babylonian hills,
and—so I guess—soon enough,
love, you and I will follow suit,
modern men, old men more or less,
one last caress by the sinkhole's
musty edge, the unheroic hospital bed.

Chancellorsville

> Let us cross over the river, and rest under the shade of the trees.
> —Stonewall Jackson's last words

Late April, the sarvisberry blossoms
fall like frayed lace. Where that fool
bullet shattered you, petals scatter
the brittle-leaf forest floor.

Today, a tourist at Chancellorsville,
I stroll the battlefield, lag by relic cases,
staring at photographs, buttons
and uniforms, the threadbare Stars and Bars

I would have fought for,
born a century sooner.
You too were a mountaineer,
from the wild hills west of here,

slopes snowy in spring with sarvis,
resurrection's first proof,
sparkling with redbud,
or the creamy dogwood bearing

Christ's rusty wounds.
Sometimes, a soldier
shrapneled with family deaths,
failed ambitions, lost lovers,

I add a slice of lemon to iced tea
and think of you, chewing lemons
even inside battle, inuring

yourself to the acids that war requires.

Here, off Route 3's roar,
I stand by the stone
that marks where you fell,
shot by your own mistaken men.

On the surgeon's table
your left arm was lost, buried
before you in a grave of its own.
If not pluck, perhaps pride

would have armed me, would have
lined me up behind you.
Perhaps I might have seized as relic
some drained lemon you tossed away,

hoping that war's chances
would allow me such courage,
such a comrade, who rests now
on the river's far bank, in the shade of the trees.

Lemon

Chess pie, whiskey sours, *tabbouleh*, sweet iced tea—
this fat lemon could have had many uses, but

here I am throwing it away untasted. It's an offering—
like silver dropped into holy wells, or Cain's insufficient

produce, or those banks of votive candles flickering
by saints' Gothic shrines. Bought for this express purpose,

tossed over the black fence-spikes onto your grave,
to join the nectarine and apple lobbed by those

who came before. Wrong fruit. They should have known.
It was lemons you loved. Any Stonewall buff knows that.

You sat the saddle and savored the sour juice, draining the fruit
while your men again and again drove the Yankees off.

Presbyterian, frugal West Virginian, you would despise
such sentimentality, such waste. *Son*, I can almost hear you chide,

*why this heathen gesture? That lemon is of no use to me.
Fetch it back. Squander none of God's gifts.* I have half a mind

to obey, but think better of clambering over the locked gate
like some overeager grave robber. A gift given to one

who cannot receive is more prayer than gift, I must admit.
I want your stubbornness, heroism, strength. I want to touch you

somehow, somehow let you know who I am, let you know
that kin are near, but, like any graveside visitor, I am far too late,

far too late. You're only a raincoat behind VMI museum glass,
a blue-eyed photo, boxed bones beneath my lemon, beneath the grass,

and this dark statue that fame, stern and enviable, set against
October's sapphire sky. Spyglasses at your side, you will not

gaze down at me, no matter how deep my desire. Instead,
you look out over Lexington, over the battlefield, into

the Valley's far distance and whatever crazed crystalline spheres
compose eternity. Sugar maples burn on the far bank, where

you stride inside the shade of the trees. We have always walked
opposite sides of that river, though that will change soon enough.

Keep the lemon, father. What else of worth have I to give except
these words, these superannuated Rebel murmurings? Glorious,

dead, you are like the weather, like this autumnal sun and breeze.
You warm us, move us, urge us, though you remain untouchable.

Weeping Freak

Oh, they would never have imagined you,
the Rebs who died, '61 to '65. You imagine
them, of course—compulsively. You read
and dream, you watch them shed exhausted
rank wool and step muscled and naked
into the Rappahannock and the James,
grabbing a quick bath in between battles.
You watch them panting in bloody piles
in Antietam's Bloody Lane, screaming
beneath the bone-saw in Shepherdstown.
You see a few locked together, bearded
young mouths kissing hard, hairy young
bodies spooning and furtively fucking
in shelter tents across the South. But they,
the common Confederate soldiers, men
you call your brothers, forebears, kin—really,
how many would not mock a mooncalf
so egregious? My God, man, look
at you. College-educated cocksucker,
redneck with highfalutin taste in booze,
sprawled shit-faced and naked in your bed,
left arm sleeved with swords and pentagrams,
C.S.A. inked into your shoulder, a beard
of gray cumulus bushing down your breast,
J.E.B. Stuart style, but he died still young,
at thirty-one, don't you know this archaic
excrescence only makes you look old?
A camo cap's cocked over your face, and,
      for fuck's sake,
big hairy man that you are, half a century

old, you're crying as you read the intro
to *Stonewall Jackson's Book of Maxims*:
        "writers of every generation since
        have asserted that had he lived,
        the Confederate States of America
        might have triumphed."
                "Shit, shit!"
you sigh, wiping your wet face,
one hundred and forty-six years
after the Battle of Chancellorsville,
ridiculous how long grief and history
linger, "Shit, shit! If only…shit!"
wishing you'd been there, heroically
to leap between Stonewall and that
mad North Carolina bullet, and did they
ever find the fool who shot him? No,
and the ball opens your lung, you've
fallen at Stonewall's feet, the staunch
Presbyterian who would surely loathe
queers, he bends to comfort the scruffy
West Virginia boy who saved him, and
you're sobbing freely now, gripping
his hand, no, God no, a man such as he
could not, would not, ever imagine you.

Cherry Picking

Early July, and the roads
are lined with cherry trees,
the limbs heavy with fruit.

We are hungry, we are weary.
Following Clubby Johnson,
our division's splashed over

the Potomac, invading
foe-country, carrying the war
all the way to Carlisle,

glared at for days by sour-
faced Pennsylvania women.
Mockingly we asked their names,

that we might write them
on paper, submerge the paper
in water, brew the purest vinegar.

Acidic the Yankee girls may be,
but not their blessed fruit trees.
No plundering of citizens,

General Lee has ordered,
but this raid we are allowed.
Some of us are barefoot,

and dusty in the summer
heat, and our canteens
are empty, so any comfort's

heaven-sent, pulling
the branches down, plucking
the ripe-red fruit, stuffing

our mouths, our haversacks,
falling out for a brief nap
in the hot orchard shade.

Now thunder rolls in the drowsy
distance. Pray for the sweet
relief of rain, cool balm sprinkling

soldiers' sun-burnt, filthy faces.
It sounds again, sky-rumble
east over South Mountain—

the very direction Heth's men rode
in search of Union shoes to steal,
a tiny town called Gettysburg.

A Few Yards of Pickett's Charge

> Up, Men, and to your posts! Don't forget today that you are from Old Virginia.
> —George E. Pickett

I try to imagine it: weight
of my musket, weight of
my cartridge box, kepi
cap cocked over my eyes,
my starved, muss-bearded
comrades on either side,
dry field grass scratching
my ankles. I manage it
just barely. And why would I
walk these few yards where
Southern bodies strode,
pride mere minutes from
death, maiming, dismem-
berment? Why, you ask,
would I picture myself
inside such a blood-
bath, try to feel what
they felt? It's a way
to honor, I suppose,
plus the mundane's never
enough for me. For
a minute or two
I want to feel fated,
glorious, heroic, I want
to believe I could—
in the face of such
suffering, such a savage
end—possess their courage.

There's Armistead,
right ahead, leading us,
hat held high on
his saber's point.
Good God, that distant
low ridge, so far away,
Cemetery Ridge, where
the Yankee guns await.
My boys marched that far,
with no shelter from
ball and shot but
the slight depression
of the Emmitsburg Road?
The chuck of lead
embedded in torsos
and heads fades,
there's only
this patient Yank
I have loved
for fourteen years
by my side, only
swallows dipping
and banking, high
grass, clumps of poison
ivy, and a few loud,
laughing tourists,
a bored adolescent
or two chatting
near the spot
where Lee rode
out to meet
his shattered
sons.

The Fourth of July

In Philadelphia,
it is given to them
to sign the document,
bewigged Northerners
and Southerners alike,
summer's heat flaking
leaves onto colonial brick.

In Washington, D.C.,
it is given to them
to slog in line through
the National Archives,
clot of tourists clamoring,
camera straps and cargo shorts,
for a chance to glimpse
the badly faded document.

In Vicksburg,
it is given to them
to surrender, after months
of siege—shells bursting
the roofs, the shelter
of caves, *in hourly dread
of snakes*, the savor
of roast mule meat, rats
bought in butcher shops,
a flavor *fully equal to that
of squirrels*, to refuse
any celebration of
Independence Day
for eighty-one years.

In Gettysburg,
it is given to them
to retreat with eight
thousand maimed
or dying, who groan
on carts without
cushions or springs,
jarring over rocky,
rutted roads, wagon
train stretching
seventeen miles in pouring
rain, the long road south,
given to them to shriek,
"Oh God! why can't I die?"
"My God, will no one
have mercy
and kill me?"
"Stop! oh!
For God's sake,
stop
just for one minute;
take me out
and leave me
to die
on
the roadside,"
while July downpour
washes blood from
the grass, while, miles
behind them, the bodies
of their comrades bloat
and rot where they fell.

In Pulaski,
it is given to us
to grow fatter

with peace, with hot
crab dip, grilled hot
dogs, broccoli salad,
Caprese salad, cole slaw,
baked beans, blueberry pie.
It is given to us to escape
such suffering, to sidestep
valor, to live and die
wispy, unmemorable, little
lives not grave enough
for history.

French Restaurant, Gettysburg

> ...all this much to gain: Pennsylvania, Maryland, the world, the golden dome of Washington itself...
> —William Faulkner, *Intruder in the Dust*

"But ma'am," I whine, a picture of alcoholic panic,
"I'm a Southerner and I just walked Pickett's Charge!
We got our asses kicked. I'm depressed. Don't
y'all have a bar? I need a martini mighty bad."

BYOB restaurant, for fuck's sake. Mysteriouser
and mysteriouser, the realms of Yankeedom.
Only complimentary wine rescues my mood
(three glasses, to be honest), and a plump hussy
near the window wearing shorts nearly short
enough to see her lady parts, a skimpy, too-tight
shirt, what kids these days would call a muffin-top,
and, oddest juxtaposition of all, an Amish bonnet
I feel compelled to mock the standard way:
"I'd like two of those, one to shit on and one
to cover it up with." Under my breath, of course,
good manners being the Southland's god.

"Those people," Lee was always calling them.
They're weird up here, it's clear; '65's victory
must have somehow warped their taste. Still,
John's rack of lamb's top-notch, as is my filet,
and there's a lemon sugar crepe for dessert
indulgence. It's a valuable distraction from

you, Armistead, hat on raised sword, leading
your Rebs over the Yankee defenses, and you,

Garnett, surely knowing what a fine target
a mounted man would be but taking that field
on horseback nonetheless, yes, intense present
sweet, this paltry pleasure's fine escape from
the past's pointless slaughters and defeats,

all you fellow Virginians, your long march
across an open meadow, thousands soaking
enemy soil in blood. There's a thin slice of
lemon garnishing the crepe, translucent as
stained glass. I tear it in half, suck on it,
eat the sour flesh the way another hillbilly
would, Stonewall, who was not here, who
might have burnt this town to the ground,
led our gray flood far past the high-water mark,
across Cemetery Ridge, east through Meade's
stubborn blue and on to smother Washington.

January Night, Johnson's Island

It is the 9th of January, 1864. It is 28 degrees below zero.

On Johnson's Island, Ohio, the prisoner-of war barracks are nothing but wooden uprights and weatherboarding, without the insulation of plaster. Through knotholes and warps, the winds whipping across Lake Erie seep, like cold streams of ocean swamping a boat.

Inside, a boy from Mobile, feverish, babbles on. "See, mama. I've picked you jasmine, and these little blue flowers like stars I found in the pasture grass. Come and let's sit on the porch and wait till twilight, till the kitchen cools and the breeze comes up from the bay. Mighty fine biscuits, mama, with this strawberry jam. Tell Sister to beware. The cottonmouth's down by the creek, the rats are in the corn crib. Here's the crock of bacon fat you asked me to fetch."

Inside, a Louisiana captain shivers and chatters, thinking of red beans and rice, brandy and bourbon, garden-rows of hot peppers and okra, the way fried oysters sputter in butter and pralines crumble beneath the teeth, the way resurrection ferns, long brittle in drought, after rain grow supple and green again. Through a crack in the wall, he watches moonlight glitter and flash on plains of lake-ice.

Inside, two officers double up in one bunk. They've been watching one another for weeks, looking for an excuse to touch, praying for necessity to conspire with desire. One's from Virginia, short and swarthy. One's from Georgia, tall and blond. They're curled together beneath doubled blankets, inside doubled body heat, the smaller man inside the bigger man's arms. Sometime in the night, the Georgian will pull the sleeping Virginian closer, then, thrilled and terrified, work a hand beneath his comrade's shirt, stroke the hair on his breast, feel a nipple's stiffness, a heart throbbing beneath his palm. The Virginian will wake, sigh, nod, nestle back against his buddy, and that throb will grow faster and harder, a young tattoo, defiant despite Scripture, despite defeat and capture and Lake Erie's ice.

In the morning, the sun will make of the lake a sapphire sheen of hardened crystal. The boy from Mobile will be dead. The Louisianan will be frozen so badly he will be unable to speak. The Virginian and the Georgian will stretch and groan. Tiny ice forming along their breath will clump their beards, glass their blankets with a fine crackle. Smiling, beneath the blanket's shelter they will squeeze hands before rising to piece together a piss-poor prisoners' breakfast of moldy salt pork and jaw-breaker hardtack.

The Battle of Cloyd's Farm

As scruffy, ragtag,
and outnumbered as their ancestors,
local boys hunker in pasture grass,
behind split-rail breastworks,

setting their rifle-sights on scary bluecoats
swarming up the hill.
Today's combat is mere theater,
but still I want to kneel

shoulder to shoulder between
that lean innocence in dirty gray
with the chinstrap whiskers
and that sturdy cub in butternut

sporting a bushy black beard.
I want to tear open a cartridge with
my teeth, taste a little gunpowder, tamp
a bullet down the barrel. Instead,

I'm aging on the sidelines,
a barrage of late April buttercups
bursting golden about my feet.
Having dispatched

two hot dogs heaped with everything,
and a bag of barbequed chips to boot,
I'm trying to glimpse what they suffered—
the hand-to-hand combat between

Virginia and West Virginia, the limbs
torn off by flying shells, the pale
flesh pierced, the panting charge,
Back Creek's waters flushed

with both sides' blood.
I'm trying to climb out
of the snarling tedia of self,
midlife pointlessness

and defeat, to step aside
into drama, May 1864,
the smoke and boom of cannon,
flare and pop of muskets, but

I'm flanked by a big-gut spectator
loudly soothing his puling child, while
all around me cell phones blather,
cameras angle, click, compete—

fly paper of the contemporary,
the banal, inescapable
for more than a few fantasized seconds—
and now it's too late

to help my bearded boys, those ferocious
Yanks once again have taken the field,
seized the artillery, scattered
the Valley's defenders. The crowd applauds,

barn swallows veer above
the victors and the vanquished.
See how simply
this war ends?

The dead and wounded rise

from trampled grass, trooping off
past the tulips' reddened ruins,
the crumpled crinolines of iris,

toward the Rebel and Union camps,
there to stoke up smoldering firepits,
polish rifles and bow
fiddles while chartreuse catkins

of the manor's oaks drift down
upon their modern bivouacs. I follow,
long enough to chat up a soldier
or two, admire here and there

a woolen derriere, peer inside
an empty tent, picturing
my aforementioned favorites there—
having stripped

off their sweat-soaked jackets,
they're lying pungent and shirtless
side by side, passing a flask, soon
to spoon away the afternoon

in bearded kisses,
sticky friction, musky naps.
Now my Yankee husbear,
his patience at an end,

elbow-tugs me back
into the present, where streams flow
bloodless, the occupying armies
of his Northern forebears

have long ago
returned to their own earth,

and Southern fields
are the South's again.

Peace awaits
just down the road:
twin rocking chairs upon the breezy
porch of Draper Mercantile,

sampling the several flavors of ice cream,
and then a drive through spring-green hills,
and then an ordinary evening at home,
bodies still blessedly intact.

The Battle of New River Bridge—Radford, Virginia

After today's grave bodily risk—
    indulging in a burger and waffle fries

despite the low-carb diet—
    after shopping for dress clothes

in this tiny railroad town once subjected
    to Federal cannon fire,

I'm strolling past frowsy
    end-of-summer jewelweed, the weary

leaves of box-elder riverside,
    trying to make you out,

trying to gauge where you stood.
    There, looming high above

Bisset Park, the modern
    bridge I have driven over uncounted

times before, and there,
    the trestle today's trains take

over the New. What I want's farther
    upriver, relics of your final battle.

I seek what was, not is.
    The high stone pillars of the wooden bridge

your Yankee comrades burnt
    in May of 1864

remain, doubling themselves in the water's
    summer-smooth mirror.

Upon the southern bank,
    where my Rebs took their stand till the stores

of ammunition ran out, I peer
    across a low river I could wade,

a high river I cannot, to the wooded ridge
    where you refused Rutherford B. Hayes'

order to take refuge in a sinkhole,
    taunting him, *in a pert and saucy way*,

"Why don't you get off your horse
    and hide too?" and "I'll get down

when you do," a few seconds before a Southern
    shell burst beside you, tearing you

into mortal shreds, and almost instant
    death discovered you to be a woman.

Sheetz in the Wilderness

Grant's just up there, upon the hill's crest,
smoking a cigar and fumbling maps. To the east,

in a field hospital beside the Wilderness Tavern,
McGuire is amputating Stonewall's arm.

To our south, that arm is buried, in Ellwood's
cemetery, where this August's corn is taller

than most men, and to our west, Confederates
are capturing Union cannon. It is difficult

to experience any of this, believe me,
what with such an absurdly long wait

for sandwiches, a Sheetz asquirm
with bus-disgorged grade-school brats.

While Sedgwick's Federals move cautiously
along the Orange Turnpike, a short, fat

Latina with oiled ringlets tugs her boyfriend's
hand and whines; he scratches his tattoos, tweaks

her breast, and pouts. Still, our surly patience
storms the line, at last achieving the war-torn

ridge-top of lunchtime, those coveted touch screens
on which I, ferocious Rebel, demand BBQ

on a whole wheat sub bun, and you, stalwart
and starvacious Yank, a club sandwich on pretzel bread,

plus the wicked luxury of curly fries (wicked,
I say, since we are always trying to diet;

it is a hard life indeed, battling
sugar, fat, alcohol, and so rarely winning.)

In Tapp Field, mere miles from here,
the Texans are shouting "Lee to the rear!"

refusing to fight further until the beloved
general is safely behind the lines,

and along the Orange Plank Road, goddamn it,
Longstreet is wounded by friendly fire just as

Jackson was only a year ago, but meanwhile
a summer storm is brewing, so,

Sheetz sandwiches bravely won,
hunger pulls us over near the battlefield's

exhibition shelter. Before us,
rain stipples the windshield, and the flames

of Saunders Field are feasting on the dead,
on wounded men trapped in smoke

and screaming. You are kind enough
to share your fries when coaxed.

Light Rain at Saunders Field

Where May muskets
　　　　　popped and smoked,
where stubble-corn
　　　　　was spattered
with the rich sap
　　　　　men's bodies make,

where Zouaves,
　　　　　surrounded,
spilled
　　　　　their exotic turbans
and stained
　　　　　their red trousers

a deeper red,
　　　　　where *men*
disappeared
　　　　　as if the earth
had swallowed
　　　　　them, where

bursting shells
　　　　　ignited dry
leaves, grass,
　　　　　and tinder-twigs,
fire swept over
　　　　　fallen soldiers

living and dead,
　　　　　where men

did their best

        to drag wounded

comrades back

        from such a char-

black fate,

        where burnt

bodies

        and, later, white bones,

lay for a year

        embriered, unburied

while the war

        moved on

without them,

        today

a light rain

        falls, late summer's

mercy sprinkled

        upon the brown-grass

earthworks

        of the Wilderness,

battlefield

        become quiet park,

rain far too late

        to stop the fires

that sprang

        from war's sharp sparks,

but still

        wetting my dry lips

and when

        I take my hat in hand,

cooling my hot

                    face, as if a friend

had dragged me

                    from a tight circle

of fire,

                    kissed my brow,

wiped blood

                    from my cheek,

and lifted a spring-

                    cold canteen to my lips.

Lee to the Rear

> As the brigade formed up in the Tapp field prior to launching a counterattack against the Northerners, Lee rode among the regiments shouting encouragement and, at one point, offering to lead them personally.
> —*Fredericksburg Battlefields*

1.
Tapp Field, August-dry,
one of few clearings in
the thick-wooded
Wilderness where one
can see sky. I walk
it fast, history-bored partner
texting in the car. A few
cannon Poague used to
drive the bluecoats back;
a marker where the Widow
Tapp's house used to be;
a replica of Troiani's painting
set in the spot where
Texas boys shouted,
"Lee to the rear! We won't
go on unless you go back!";
and two markers for those
Texas boys themselves,
of whom two-thirds fell
in that rushing assault.
The few tears I allow
myself these tranquil days
wedged in between past
and future sorrows fanged fate
decrees I save for memorials
such as these, for passions,

youths, and losses long
past. The present grows
flat, it moves me little,
and I myself prove
less and less
significant.

2.
The Rebel army nearly shattered
here, driven in by Hancock's men,
before Longstreet's reinforcements
rushed up just in time and Gregg's
Texans drove the blue offensive
back. In Don Troiani's painting,
"Lee's Texans," the Rebel battle flag
looks gnawed, as if by some ravenous
serpent. Upon Traveller's muscled
gray, Lee lifts his hat, ready to lead
the army on, ready to fall in the fore-
front if necessary. "Go back,
General Lee, go back!" they shout,
men from Austin, San Antonio,
God knows what tiny Texas towns
they will never see again. Hands surge
forward. In another second, a boy
named Gee will seize Traveller's
bridle and lead Lee back behind
the lines while his Lone Star fellows
tear forward with a cheer and drive
the foe back toward the Brock Road,
delaying defeat yet again, yet again.

3.
Leonard Groce Gee.
From Velasco. A widower

now, age seventy-one.
I was twenty-six then. May '64,
a field in northern Virginia,
a quick movement of my hand,
leather seized, soft against my palm,
and history seized as well.
"Texans always move them!"
Lee shouted, and we swelled
with pride at such words.
"I want every man of them
to know I am here with them,"
he told Gregg, but we knew
he was with us always,
he loved us all, and we loved
him nearly as steadily as
we love God, and so we had
to have him sheltered, safe,
for—oh, God forbid, blood
in that gray beard? Who
could have fought without him?
Our father, we would have
followed him anywhere, like
a comet, like the colors,
like a votive candle, but
that day he followed me, I led
his mount behind Poague's guns,
and he thanked me there, took
my hand and called me
Dear son. Perhaps he cursed
me later, at Appomattox, or during
the bitter subjugation after, when
he might have ached for death,
but I want to believe he thanked
me again, remembering my sun-
brown face and murmuring,
"Hurrah for Texas!" that burning

October of 1870, those last days
among Lexington's maples, as he lay
dying and his sons by the thousands,
we all passed the bed of
his delirium, he shook
the hands of boys both living
and dead, then closed
his eyes and left us
with far less reason to love.

The Sweet Studs of Spotsylvania

It's pouring rain over Spotsylvania,
the latest of nearly one hundred and fifty years'
worth of thunderstorms both savage and gentle,
all leaching more deeply still into black Virginia dirt
what blood might linger, the mingled molecules
of blue and gray spilled here, the mortal rilling
and gushing evoked by artillery shell and Minié ball.
I'm dry as yet, spared by timing from both wet
and warfare, having fled beneath the exhibit shelter.
Waiting out the deluge, I'm besotted again, gazing
into today's young ranger's blue eyes and musing
on Plato. *The Symposium* gave me hope that
one fine day I might move beyond the agonized
(i.e., irrepressibly horny yet for the most part celibate)
yearning for individual men and glow like tamped fire
with more sublime passions, for philosophy, morality,
science, knowledge. Dutifully I've striven to abandon
Erato, muse of love poetry, for her more mature
and sober sister, Clio, muse of history. Thus
my presence here, where Grant's men hammered
the Rebel salient, but, as you can see, I backslide
at the slightest provocation, today's tempting show—
only yards from the spot where Sedgwick fell—
being this ranger's brown beard and lashes,
the curly chest hair my furtive glance can glean
above his uppermost shirt button. I'm expert
at feigning fascination with the walking tour
pamphlet my latest ardor hands me while indulging
in a few hearthside log-cabin fantasies recycled
from my forestry-major youth—and wouldn't

he be warm, cuddly, and so sweetly submissive?
What makes this world fallen? It does not oblige
my every passing lust. I'm hungry for an unseemly
hug, but that way misdemeanor lies. Instead, before
darting out into downpour, I'm sure to shake his hand.

♦

Here was the heaviest fighting, the Bloody Angle,
breastworks heaped high, taken and retaken
in a rain as wild as today's. Cursed with wet
gunpowder, my Rebs went at them hand to hand,
bayonets shoved through sides, musket butts
swung against foe-skulls, holey brogans sliding
in the treacherous slip of mingled mud and blood.
Little here now but this field across which Yankees
swarmed, low lines of bunched earth like great mole-
tracings, ditches where my sweaty soldiers sheltered
between rifle-rounds, and forest—summer-dense,
wind-thrashed, scourged by hard rain, silvery
leaves belly up—where once the Rebel army held firm.
Were I blessed with more than human clarity,
I could discern several thousand ghosts, leaning
on their arms, bloody-bearded, glaring at my
safety, sentimentality, and softness. I could shiver
endlessly, freezing over every spot where a man fell.
Insularity spares me: the flesh, the year, the self I'm
thoroughly immured inside. Still, I'm about to hazard
the field—"Tour Stop 3: 2nd Corps Attacks"—when
lightning and the roar of thunder unlimbered
drive me back. Two specters there, moving
my way along a line of trees? No, two handsome
strangers beneath an umbrella as wide and streaming
as mine. Wiry-built honeys, they're looking for
the Bloody Angle. We bend together over rain-
wrinkled pamphlets, umbrellas bumping, beards

nearly brushing; I lead them along the earthworks,
past the spot where incessant fire reduced
a great oak to a stump. Here, here, I say, trying
to focus on history, not lust, yet ambushed again:
a chestnut beard / friendly, a black beard / aloof.
They're from Chattanooga, teachers on vacation.
I imagine them dressed in Confederate gray,
then shirtless, then naked, then hogtied POW's.
I want to ask which one's the Top—much preferring
to see the haughty dark one pounded from behind.
I'm tempted to suggest that such fortuity, bumping
into them on a battlefield, in a violent lightning storm,
might mean that we three fought here side by side
in our last lives, might mean that, after snogging
in the car, we should find a warm hotel room
to take a friendly shower and make a Daddy-
sandwich, but I fear I'm too old to inspire erotic
interest, and, young as they are, they're most
likely monogamous—quaint, romantic habit—
and, God, besides, even in my own youth I was
never bold enough to make such a risky pass.
I give them hearty handshakes—stealing again
what meager skin-to-skin I can—before walking
us through shared storm to separate cars, to
small lives the present permits us, the riveting
trivia of lust, amusement, ambition, while this summer's
rain sluices past blood deeper. Plato, Clio, Erato,
I've changed little, if at all, other than an easy weeping
for long-ago losses not my own. Goodbye, sweet studs
of Spotsylvania. History, let's face it, is only a stage set
of sorrowful facts inside which I imagine men like you:
the beauties that came before, the heroes I never met.

Making Love To Stuart

Beware! This is what comes
of permitting homosexuals to read
history. We're all hungry for
drama, that prized conjunction
of the erotic and heroic
that has fueled so many television
mini-series. Thus I savor
sweet and sweaty wild nights,
wild nights making love to Stuart.
Who could resist the flair,
the cavalier cap complete
with feather, who could resist
the ride around McClelland?
Most especially, who could resist
this foxtail beard, chestnut-
brown bush he runs over my face
and down my torso? Christ.
Fur of the same color dusts
his belly, soon to be bullet-split
at Yellow Tavern, and lines
the crevice between smooth-
plump butt-curves I stroke,
pushing my face between them,
one tentative flick of the tongue
before his wife Flora, played by
Miss Sue Ellen Ewing of erstwhile
Dallas fame, throws open the door,
and so I leave my lover Jeb un-
eaten, unplucked, unfucked,

leaping out the window like
Don Juan, only to wake up panting
beside my snoring husbear.

Jeb Stuart in the Suburbs

> He told me he never expected to live through the war, and that if we were
> conquered, that he did not want to live.
> —Jeffry D. Wert, *Cavalryman of the Lost Cause: A Biography of J.E.B. Stuart*

You never knew his name,
the Yank from Michigan who shot you
down during the Battle of Yellow Tavern.
The ball opened your flank, pierced
your stomach. It took you a day
to die, muttering, "I am resigned;
God's will be done." Only thirty-one,
gone before your wife could make it
to your side. Beauty, magnificently
bewhiskered one, I am glad to report,
with that partisan rage I cannot quite
slough off just yet, that your slayer
was shot down mere weeks later.
Today, there's no Yellow Tavern left,
only ever-expanding Richmond,
the city you lost your life to save,
traffic whizzing or creeping along
smelly interstates. Today, there are
only trimmed suburbs, brick ranch
houses, pink crepe myrtle bushes,
and a quiet grove of hollies about
this obelisk monument where you fell.
Beneath the mourning dove's sad coo,
earlier pilgrims have left their offerings:
a cavalry hat, a miniature plastic
horse and rider, the letters CSA
cut out in cardboard, a couple of tiny

Stars and Bars. How you would
savor such attentions, the thought
of being so admired decades after
your death. To live with honor,
to die in battle, to be remembered!
Yes, I know that archaic craving,
that foolish and manly ambition.
You got what you dreamed of:
glory, then a death that spared you
defeat. If you loved poetry and romance
as well as books suggest, you will
forgive me if fancifully I imagine
you here, stretched out on the grass,
dozing in the shade, cavalier hat
tilted over your face, the fiery
auburn beard I would so have loved
to stroke bushing upon your breast.

Cherry Petals, VMI

They fell in a field far from here,
on a day of thunder, sky roaring
over cannon, cannon snarling back.

257 VMI cadets
rushing forward in the doubled
darkness of smoke and downpour

across a farm north of New Market,
through the white snow of apples,
grove of fruiting become history's

fatal orchard, pink cheeks waning white,
corpses plastered with mud and petals.
These ten brought down were too young,

all under twenty-five. Over them leans
"Virginia Mourning Her Dead,"
the great statue of a sorrowing Athena,

and set together within a copper box
beneath the goddess' feet, like harvest
the bones of boys are gathered in.

Sad father, I summon them,
running my fingers over etched names,
the smooth marble of grave markers—

Atwill, Cabell, Crockett; Hartsfield,
Haynes; Jefferson, Jones, McDowell;

Stanard, Wheelwright—

as does the Corps still, ceremony
held on the anniversary of the battle,
each name met with this answer:

"Died on the Field of Honor, sir."
That battle, that day, that May, long gone.
It's 2011, and April yet, nearly a century

and a half later, and my partner and I—
middle-aged, no warriors—are visiting
VMI for a garden tour. Today,

Southern ladies so like my mother
have filled crystal bowls and vases
with lilacs, roses, sweet shrub, presiding

over punch and lemon bars, in rooms
where Jackson and Maury moved.
Today, polite white-clad cadets pass us

with greetings and smiles, one with an ass
so round and tight John almost stumbles—
"You could bounce a quarter off it,"

he mutters. Today, this huge cherry tree
is hung with Housman's snow, but pink,
pink, great furbelows of pink already

unraveling—God, every apex is only
an instant—drifting with the breeze,
scurrying about the great statue's base,

pink snow flaking across the graves,
highlighting then concealing names.

Fingers stroking a cheek, confetti tossed

in a victory parade, a lady's tear-wet
handkerchief, bits of bloodstained bandage?
No, simply a new generation

of loveliness ashrivel, organics browning
at the edges, across the letters sacrifice
cut into nerveless, deathless stone.

Cold Harbor

> It was not war, it was murder.
> —Evander Law

June the third, 1864. In Virginia,
June is the sweetest month,
mixing morning mist with
deepening green. The night
before the battle, Federal hopes
were deciduous, men *calmly writing*
their names and home addresses
on slips of paper and pinning
them to the backs of their coats
so that their bodies might be
recognized and their fate made
known to their families at home.

Today, last insects chirp cool
October afternoon, cloudless
quartz-crystal facets, rich
with the scent of resin.
First I stand behind the low
hill and ditch of Confederate
earthworks, where my Rebs
in thirty minutes shot down
seven thousand Federal foes.
The field cauldron-seethed,
Grant's great blue tide broke
and weltered, a choppy
pool of dead and wounded
left to please the vultures, left

to rot and moan for three days
before flags of truce were raised.

Now the driving-tour route loops
us bloodlessly across that same
field emptied of all but dying
grass and pine trunks reptile-
barked and so on to the enemy

works, where tourist
curiosity might safely stand
where so many pushed off,
like a diver off a board, like
a runner at the start, racing
into oblivion sweetly swift
for some, slower, far slower
for others, seven thousand
chairs up North left vacant,
seven thousand families
creped in mourning black.

Across that slaughter-field,
autumn sun's soft brass
on glossy fallen foliage.
Its light makes gleam
of the oaks' last hold-outs, dead
leaves that cling to twigs,
resist the wind, will not
let go. This shard of black
carbon beneath my boot
I could use to char-scrawl
my husband's name, my own.
See the last bit of campfire,
embers dwindled down
with dawn? Hear a boy

who cannot read or write
ask the handsome messmate
he's come to adore please
to pen his name, please
to help him pin the paper
safe inside his jacket.

A Roughed-Up Redneck

Tonight, buzzed on cheap wine, blessed
and naked on a living room floor in Salem,
Virginia, he's licking boots into wet ebony
glisten. Now a thick knob of leather's buckled
in his mouth; now he's doubled up, bolted
steel restraints locking wrists to ankles.
His captor hangs Japanese clover clamps from
his nipples, twists and tugs the chain between
till groans well and rise like campfire smoke.
When a pair of piss-and-cum-rank briefs is
draped over his face, he snuffles the thick
scent as eagerly as a bear would a broken hive.
The boy needs to hurt, needs the heavy anchor
of helplessness, needs the reassurance
of a leather strap to unearth dull damson
bruises on his hairy pecs and back, this goateed
mountain boy drooling around his gag, sobbing
and rapt,
          and this morning, clean, so clean,
driving down back roads lined with April's
gleaming new green, purple irises, redbud
and lilacs burning on farmhouse lawns,
along the base of Hanging Rock Mountain,
where Jubal Early routed the Yanks, last
Confederate victory in the Valley, this son
of those distant Rebels, this willingly
roughed-up redneck, driving a rusting
pickup truck, CSA tattoo and aching nipples
beneath an Everlast sweatshirt, humming
and grinning to country music, clean
and light as leaves after a night's hard rain.

After The Reenactment 1

I worry about these dead,
Rebel soldiers lying in the rain-
sodden grass of Cedar Creek.
They have lain there long,
this miserably wet October day,
slumped against the pasture-
grass, the hard chill of earth,
in their premature deaths,
in the awkward collapse and splay
of men downed by shell and ball.
But now that blue-clad shrimp
Sheridan has driven off my man
Early, the battle's over—abrading
that, year after year, it always ends
the same, we Rebs routed—
so now the corpses rise
stiffly, slowly, as they must do
in all those scenes depicting
Judgment Day. The blond boy
who died in 1864
ruefully pats the hole in his side
and gets to his knees, contemplating
that long walk back to Georgia.
The cannoneer with the thick arms
and a scruffy beard the red-gold
of mountain sunsets, half his face
shot off, he's rubbing now his renewed
lips and cheek, ready to head
home to Franklin County, where
hot biscuits with apple butter await.

And I, I cock my redneck cap against
the drizzle's persistence, shake off
the shivers, and contemplate
dinner options in Winchester,
wishing my boys big meals
and warm beds tonight, snuggling
spouses, and an escape from
the bad colds and pneumonia,
the nightmares that might
result from lying so long,
so meticulously unmoving,
in the bitter arms of rain and earth.

After The Reenactment 2

After the battleground's bitter cold, the conflict at Cedar Creek
fought and lost yet again, after shepherd's pie and martinis,

pumpkin cheesecake, the bushy-bearded redneck in rawhide
jacket, Stonewall Jackson cap, and lumberjack boots who

cheered the Rebs on all rainy afternoon is naked, sprawled
in a broad bed, listening to storm stroke the windows of

Winchester's Fairfield Inn. He's grinning with the perverse
pleasure of juxtaposition, to be of his region and so much not,

his husband tugging his nipples and stroking his C.S.A.
tattoo while his husband's new boyfriend sits on his cock.

♦

Allen of the smooth and loverly curvaceous butt
sleeps beside me, and John of the furry curvaceous
butt beside him. Most sweet. I'm guessing that
this is a first in history, a gay three-way following
a Civil War reenactment, but of course I'm not
the only bearded butt-pirate obsessed with the War
of Northern Aggression. I lie here beside my softly
snoring boys, and softly the rain persists, ticking
the panes like some overactive clock. Turner,
I can't sleep, thinking of you there, just across town.
The rain runs over your skull, fondles your ribcage
in Stonewall Cemetery, where you lie, Black Knight
of the Confederacy, beside the brother you could

not save. Buddy, you were just the sort I dote on:
short, dark, wiry, muscled, reckless, black beard
flowing over your breast. I would have been one
of many willing to follow you anywhere, though
partisan patriotism would have been hard-spined
with less noble motives, it is true. Adored even
after you fell at Chestnut Ridge, your sword
and spurs were stolen, relics made of your horse's
tail, your corpse's beard gone missing half a foot.
Dead like Christ at thirty-three, you would be
182 years old tonight. Damn wide ravine, bridged
only one way. Unmarried, never engaged, did
a man supposedly such an epitome of chivalry
die a virgin? Take on flesh, Turner. Slip in here,
hero, between the sheets. Let me warm you,
your back snuggled against my chest. Let black
beard and gray goatee mingle till dawn. Hairy
beauty, bravery, let me show you how a man's
body is blessed. Let me caress your torso's hard
and grassy Shenandoah hills, kiss the wound
in your blood-stained breast. Sad little brother,
Centaur of the South, teach me how to ride.

Sheridan Circle

> Fort Scammon—At the top of the hill is the site of an earthwork fort built by Union soldiers in 1863. During the battle of Sept. 13, 1862, Confederate artillery fired on Charleston from this place. Hayes and McKinley, future presidents, served at the fort.
> —West Virginia Historical Marker

I knew none of it then.
Sheridan was a smudgy memory,
a note taken in high-school history class.
Past Hayes Avenue, up McKinley:
123 Sheridan Circle was affordable,
a split-level on Fort Hill, with fine
views out over Charleston, dusk
a great bowl of urban glitterings.
We relished the fireplace in winter,
the back patio in summer, made many
a friend many a plumping meal.
In the downstairs den we watched
DVD's, lifted weights. In the tiny office,
on our iMac I composed vampires
and Norse warriors, worried about
tenure, tied up a big-chested boy
or two. In the afternoons, I often
took an hour's walk, down to the hill's
base, past the historical marker I rarely
read, then up the long spiraling incline
to the top, to that circle of earthworks
where something significant, irrelevant,
happened, Confederates first, then
later Union troops. In the center was
a fetid pool, once a well, I suppose.
I did not imagine long-dead soldiers

drinking from that water, or shouldering
muskets, waiting stiffly for the foe's
approach. Instead, I scrambled up
the grassy parapets, strolled along
the tops. What little was left of that
fort was all very much like a doughnut
of soil; it was a pleasant spot to walk.
War had occurred long ago, it was there
waiting for me in many a book, but
in my head it had not happened yet.
Grant had not yet ordered Sheridan
to leave the Valley *so bare that
a crow flying over it would be
compelled to carry his rations.*
Smoke had not yet shut out the sun,
women were not yet screaming
and tearing their hair while bonfires
kindled from Virginia home and
Virginia mill and Virginia barn spit
sparks like fiery phlegm into the face
of autumn sky. 1864 had not yet
arrived. I stroked high summer
grass as I passed. I breathed in
clear air, albeit sometimes scented
with Kanawha Valley industry.
I inhaled a sweet, shallow innocence,
a comfortable autobiography,
seemingly free, as yet, of history.

Shep—December 1864

To continue
through it,
in tattered brogans
marching over brambles,
rocky razors, leaving
bloody footprints
along the snowy roads,
to continue
despite the worm-
infested crackers,
the slimy beef,
the mule meat,
ink freezing
on a pen, ink made
of oak galls and poke-
berries, a letter
scrawled home,
nothing but us
between the enemy
and home,
to continue
for honor, for kin,
for tonight's stag dance,
my little fellow, my
little Virginian,
my chicken, as
the boys call him,
Brendan swaying
and flushed in fire-
light, grinning in

my arms, all night
frost and flurry,
our snug nest of oil-
cloth and pine straw,
his back pressed against
my chest till dawn, to
continue through
the whine of blue-
coat ball, the claw
of lice and flea,
chewing the last of
the horses' corn
we break between
stones, to continue
past futility, past the thought
of suffering for naught—
sick for Georgia and
God, those fried
peach pies, to continue
for Brendan's beard
so soft beneath
my fingers—what we do
alone at night no man
needs to know, oh God,
how I ride the boy,
his groans grown loud
beneath my clamped
palm, my lips upon
his temple, shushing,
shushing, his nether grip
so tight I'm quick to
spend—yes, there are men
who fight for hate's
sake, and I can see that,
having heard the name
Sherman, but I continue

now for love, dodging
bullets, praying each
twilight my little man
is spared another day,
I continue for our
next shared night
and, God willing,
a farmhouse together
in Highland County
after the war is won
or done.

Shep—Prayer After the Great Snowball Battle

> It was probably the greatest snowball battle ever fought, and showed that "men are but children of larger growth."
> —John O. Casler, *Four Years in the Stonewall Brigade*.

Even in the prevailing peace
of winter quarters, we Rebel
troops will fight. With no
Yanks to drive, our divisions
take on each other, patting
snowballs into shape, piling
them in white cairns, lobbing
them toward the friendly foe.
Brendan, my beloved little
lad, his eyes glinting blue—
his breath's a swirl of gauze,
his auburn-whiskered smile
ice-edged, his aim dead-true.
The drums beat the long roll,
the fifes shrill, the colors fly,
as if our combat were real,
as if those cold balls were hot
grape and lead slamming into
the wool-muffled bodies of
grown-up boys, as death most
surely will come the spring.
But not today, our army
swaddled in thickening snow
and winter's cease-fire safety.
Watching my gleeful lad,
I cannot help but pray
and tremble. Lord, let us last

into triumph and a full life
after, my chicken and I,
into shared old age. Let us
live to remember the youths
we were, live to remember
this afternoon in February
near Orange Court House,
when war became not bitter
truth but laughing sham,
when chuckling Brendan stole
a stand of colors, when
our division claimed victory
as night fell over the camp,
and, inside our tiny cabin,
we eased ourselves out
of slush-soaked uniforms,
blocked the door, stoked
up the fire, split stale biscuits,
bacon-savory bean soup,
then blew out the candle-stub
and naked Brendan shared
my bed, his strength curled
and sighing inside mine,
bucking beneath my weight—
God, his hairy hills and caves,
his musky beard, his salty
sex, firm breast, sweet tongue—
how hard and close we slept
inside a matchless warmth.
May our shared heat—if
Thy will permit—outlast
the cough and flux of winter,
survive this war's razor-
sabered seasons. Lord,
quilt our bodies in Thy mercy.

v.

Lexington Busboy

What are you doing here, Turner Ashby,
fourteen decades dead, Rebel hero I've come to love?
College-aged today, dressed all in black, yet I know
your jet-dark hair, the hue mine used to be, I see you
inside the thick bangs, black sideburns and goatee
of this beautiful boy bussing the table beside me,
clearing dirty glasses, forks, and plates, swift and neat
as you once swept Yankees from Virginia's Valley.
You're short and solid as before, though in this time
tattoos spill from your left sleeve, silver hoops
glint in your ears. No matter; even lovelier.
You're hirsute beneath that shirt, I can tell from here.
My hotel's near, boy. Follow me; surrender. You're
the god I strip and bind. You're rebirth rough and tender.

Escaping Chimborazo

Imagination is, as usual, an inefficient sieve-net,
despite the short film about Civil War medicine
and the Confederate hospital of Chimborazo,
a small city of barracks that once stood where
we stand, inside this post-bellum mansion
turned museum, on a breezy plateau just east
of downtown Richmond. We bend to the exhibits—
a model of the camp, photographs of doctors
and nurses, the horrible instruments of
the amputation kit—text hard to read in
the dim light and through the chatter of some
garrulous cow in the foyer who's hell-bent to share
with the ranger on duty every banal bit of gossip
she can muster. They remain gray outlines,
translucent as satin glass, the men who lay—
after Gaines Mill, Malvern Hill, Cold Harbor,
and Petersburg—in ranked lines of beds, who
thrashed and screamed, who lay in supine
swoons as sharpened bone saw and trepan
screw served necessity, as grim-jawed attendants
disposed of shattered limbs, bloodstained clothes,
bits of skull and brain.
                        Again and again, golden
Yank, through the years we've shared, I lead
your patience into gray shades that haunt me,
past relics of blood, death, and horror one hundred
and fifty years have failed to forget, and you—
descendant of my former foes—have never once
complained. Saturated with wounded ghosts,
we leave the saw teeth and scalpels, stepping

out into the scent of blooming crepe myrtles
and a blue vista over the summer James.
In five minutes, we're sloughing off the past,
its maiming, its gray phlegms and gangrenes,
at the counter of Proper Pie Company, mere yards
from the church where Edgar Allan Poe's mother lies
and Patrick Henry balanced liberty and death.
The staff's friendly, a crew of tattooed and pierced
hipsters, full of young laughter and smiles. The hot
bearded boy who serves us, we tacitly decide, would
look best naked and sandwiched between us. Let's sit
together in amused lust and twenty-first-century
sunlight, savoring strong coffee and coconut cream pie,
the bustle of the present, your solid knee bumping mine.

The Death Of Beautiful Men

For years I've sought you, fellow Virginian,
literary kin, in places you once knew,
historic spaces memorializing your name:

your mother's grave in St. John's churchyard;
West Range Number Thirteen, the room
assigned to you during that brief stint

as a student at UVA, where you broke up
and burnt your furniture for warmth; your statue atop
Richmond's Capitol Hill; the Old Stone House

Poe Museum, prized relics of your walking
stick and a snipped lock of hair; Hiram
Haines' Coffee House in Petersburg,

where you and Virginia Clemm spent your honey-
moon; and finally, in Baltimore, that ornate
tomb set over your soil-shrouded corpse,

the sculpture's every niche wedged with coins
left by the superstitious and the admiring.
I designate Beauty as the province of the poem,

you proclaimed, and Melancholy *the most
legitimate of all the poetical tones.*
How lovely they were to you, those emaciate maidens,

hyacinthine Ligeia wasting away,
pallid Madeline Usher too early entombed.
You mourned by the vault of Ulalume when the leaves

were ashen and sere; you lay down by the side of your bride
Annabel Lee in her sepulchre there by the sounding
sea; you sought surcease of sorrow for the lost

Lenore, by a black-plumed demon denied
nepenthe. *The death, then, of a beautiful woman is,
unquestionably, the most poetical topic*

in the world, you conclude. I fear, darksome brother,
against this aesthetic definition I must
demur. Who knows what god or Weird decides

where or when a man finds beauty?
For you, those fragile ladies—neurasthenic,
consumptive, most bewitching in their vanishing.

For myself, the virile, heroic, manly. Here,
the death of beautiful men.
                            Magnificent
Hector, stabbed through the neck, slumps and gasps.

Dying, he knows all he loves will fall
through his failure. Dead, his body's dragged
across the plain, sprawling useless in the dust.

Blood stains the unmoving swell of his chest,
the sticky thicket of his beard. Here, the scruffy
King of the Jews, roped to a pillar and flogged,

bare and sweaty flank spear-pierced,
left to sag upon the killing tree.
Here, Ashby, leading Confederate cavalry,

musket-shot through the heart, scarlet welling
from his tautly muscled torso like hot springs
through hirsute grass. Or your hometown, Richmond,

whose fall you were spared by early death. Sixteen
years after they found you dying on the streets
of Baltimore, the city writhed in flame, the Yanks

ripped down from the Capitol the Stars and Bars,
hoisted up the Stars and Stripes. Here's
one of the South's last defenders—a dark-

bearded soldier of twenty, belly slit
at Petersburg by a Northern bullet only
a week before four years of war

are fated to end—panting pained breaths
in Chimborazo's musty hospital wards.
No one knows his name, no one loves him

here but I. The boy's baby-faced,
eyes lustrous with delirium. I brush mussed
bangs from his fever-hot brow, tip

a cup of water to his lips. He's shirtless,
thick black chest hair glistening
with sweat. Resting a hand upon his breast,

I mark how his heart's elegiac tide recedes.
I stroke his cheek, clasp his callused hand,
lie by his side, easing him into merciful sleep.

Tomorrow's prayer and shoveled soil. Poe,
we know the poet's perverse fate and cost—
our love's most ardent for what's irretrievably lost.

The Fall Of Richmond

From a drunken couch-crash, too much Mezcal
in the Fan, his host wakes him an hour
before dawn with the offer of a joint,
then straddles his chest and shoves the hard
lump beneath briefs into his face. Too drained
to care, acquiescent guest, he closes his eyes
and opens his mouth. Beginning to suck,
he wishes himself atop some solitary
Matterhorn with the imp he loved
and lost, far out of this era in which the dew
of pearls is poisonous. Hands grip
his shaven head and pull him closer.

♦

This train is bound for Danville Station.
Davis sits backwards, watching Richmond's
lights drift off like exhausted fireflies,
like wind-scattered bivouac sparks.
This last midnight about the Capitol
simmers with azaleas. The train jerks,
jerks, then shudders out over the river-bridge.
One last whistle. Nobility closes its eyes.

♦

Beneath the tailored winter coat his nipples
are bruised, his groin is honeycomb
emptied, wax squeezed flat, maple tapped
out. The weather's moodily accommodating,

macabre clouds and a steady rain, steady as
the rapids of the James filling Hollywood
Cemetery with oracular hush. The magnolias
are ancient, with obese buds. The grave
of Jefferson Davis is flanked with witness,
marble angels. To the wet black bark
of magnolia and of holly he presses
his hands, his rope-reddened wrists,
as if memory could be absorbed, or heroism.

♦

Boxes of documents are dumped
on the street, paper scraps
and the stink of kerosene lift
the night with spiral columns.
In Shockoe Slip, tobacco warehouses
burn like forsythia banks—the Yanks
will retrieve nothing save foundation
stone and char.

♦

Each Christmas-party guest must beg
for a gingerbread dog bone. The bartender
is harnessed and shirtless, windows
left open to keep his nipples erect.
Our hero in leather vest and black boots
is cross-eyed with Absolut, bending
to sniff white freesias, white tulips,
white gardenias floating in a glass bowl
flanked by white candles, delicious
and sickening as a stranger's semen,
as touch without touch.

♦

Now the black oil of the James ignites,
the ironclads explode, the powder magazine—
infectious azaleas. All over Richmond,
window glass shatters. Elegance
has become a scrap of velvet
mud pastes to a soldier's shoe-sole.

◆

Time for the gag gifts—dildos,
dog collars, condoms, more dildos.
More vodka, please. Moron, he always falls
in love with men who leave.
To take the bartender's biceps between
his teeth, that might help. Instead,
Mother Christmas appears, lip-syncs
Dolly's "I Will Always Love You"
with electric bees circling in her
white gossamer hive of a wig.

◆

Spastic as rodents, the mob seizes kegs
of whiskey and breaks them open on
the streets. Across the bricks the liquor rolls
like black waves eroding shingle. Men fall
to their knees, shouting, scoop and lap
it up, then reel off to loot abandoned shops.

◆

In the bathroom, too drunk, Roman
with a feather, he puts a finger down
his throat. Rinses his beard, grinds
a thumb conveniently numb into

a candle flame, snuffs the wick,
adjusts his dick, weaves up
to the panoramic rooftop deck.

◆

Wind is always waiting to spread
a flame, to rush an arsenal. The shells
explode all night, as if the enemy
had already arrived. Dawn's a creak
of wagons. Blue uniformity
at the city gates means for America
slavery and aristocracy are over,
means the sun's sulphurous yolk
will rise in a choke of smoke. Gray
is the marriage of extremes, gray
is the color of ash.

◆

Thank God the wind is bitter here,
rustling the dead potted pampas grass,
carrying off the beloved name he mutters,
vodka-sentimental, the name of a saint,
a cloud of breath and of defeat. The lit
skyline of Richmond's a clump
of tombstones. The wax on his thumb
he nibbles off like congealed cum;
the cloud-ceiling glows above
as if reflecting fire.

Belle Isle Prison Camp

The tents are long gone.
In photos taken during the war,
they proliferate like white tepees,
Ku Klux Klan masks, children
clad in ghostly sheets clamoring
for trick-or-treat chocolates,
but now, where the prison camp
once was, there are only a scraggly
plain and bike paths, October grass
taller than I, and, directly above
my head, the rumble of the highway,
Route 301 crossing the James, great
pylons of the Robert E. Lee Bridge
I walk between, as if through
a triumphal arch or around
the ankles of a colossus.

◆

Bare then. No trees that might obstruct
the aim of guards atop the island's hill,
cannon to prevent any thoughts of escape,
rebellion, disorder. No barracks, simply
tents. Three thousand tents, eventually
ten thousand Union prisoners. From here,
aching for their homes in Ohio, New York,
Pennsylvania, Indiana, all they could see
was the rocky, swirling river, and, beyond
that flow, Richmond's church spires, and,
atop its grand prominence, the neoclassical
Capitol building Thomas Jefferson designed.

◆

In warmer months prisoners were allowed
to bathe in the swift waters of the James.
The weakest sat in the sandy shallows,
trying not to sob, resting their heads
in their hands. A desperate few threw
themselves into the rushing current, there
to be shot, swept up into the rapids,
dashed against rock-jags and drowned.
Only a handful crawled gasping up
the far bank, stopped for breath, dread
already estimating the long miles north.

◆

We are laying on Belle Isle with no tents or blankets.
Plenty of body lice here.
Laying out on the ground.
Still laying out on the ground.

◆

A good deal of fighting going on among the men.
Just like so many hungry wolves penned together.

◆

Rations half a loaf of some kind of stuff,
I don't know what to call it.
It is cobs all ground up and raw,
also half a pint of rice.

I saw one of the prisoners gather up
what one of them vomited, wash it off,

*cook it again and eat it. Starvation
will make us do anything.*

◆

*While on Belle Isle the rations were so meager
and of such poor quality, that anything
in the shape of food was eagerly sought after.
The officer in immediate command
at the time was the owner of a fine pointer dog
that came inside the prison frequently
in company with his master. So it occurred
to a member of the 13th Indiana
and Comrade Lienberger that they would
make the attempt to capture and kill that dog,
and thus procure food. Watching
their opportunity they allured the dog
into their excuse for a tent, when they suddenly
threw a blanket over him to stifle his cries, and,
while Lienberger held the dog's hind legs,
the Indiana man succeeded in cutting his throat.
They dressed the carcass, selling some
of the meat and giving some away, still
retaining a good share for themselves.*

◆

Both sides took up arms
with broad-shouldered ideals.
God was on their side, no doubt.
Union! Defense of kin and home!
Can those be men? asked Walt Whitman,
seeing prisoners released from Belle Isle.
*Those little livid brown, ash streaked,
monkey-looking dwarves? — are they not
really mummified, dwindled corpses?*

He might have said the same of Yanks
limping from Andersonville and Libby,
prisoners the half-starved South
could not afford to feed, or Rebs
released from Camp Chase, Elmira,
Johnson's Island, prisoners the North
could well have fed but did not.
Half-dressed, emaciated, withered
with frostbite, scurvy, exposure, the flux.
War would make them warriors.
War would make them infants.

◆

Had I thought of it, I might have
brought a picnic—bread and cheese,
perhaps, or even a surreptitious
flask. Belle Isle's a city park now,
a few quiet, wooded acres the rocky
river skirts, a leafy calm one flees
not from but to, retreat from Richmond's
busy urban ruckus. Bikers flash by,
and here and there a jogger, a few
muscled sets of hairy thighs, young
men who would make fine soldiers,
and now here comes a grade-school
group, unruly horde of children on
some field trip, hyperactive with
delight, having escaped the classroom
for a few morning hours this warm
October day. They mill in the sun
like minnows, their shouts driving
the songbirds out, too young, as yet
too undamaged to care who suffered
here and how. I leave them stomping
and swirling where white tents

rotted and soldiers froze to death.
Where there was silence, they
bring their screaming, punishing
the air, the autumn. They will not
stop, they scream and kick the earth,
they will not stop their screaming.

"Dixie"

> Campaigns against "Dixie" and other Confederate symbols have helped create a sense of political ostracism and marginalization among working-class white Southerners.
> —Wikipedia, "Dixie" (song)

Today's workshop poem contains
Virginia rednecks, a pickup truck,
the Confederate flag, and "Dixie,"
all of which the first-person speaker
excoriates with eye-rolling vigor.

Yes, the song's repugnant, my students
sternly inform me, every one of them
nodding in sleek agreement. Forget
the lyrics; the mere melody's enough
for outrage, a backwards racist tune

> *I wish I were in the land of cotton*

beloved of poor white trash, a series
of notes no one should play for fear
of giving offense. When I mention
my Rebel ancestor and gently suggest
that not everyone feels as they do,

their faces are expressionless,
a tacit tallying-up of my boots and bushy
beard, tattoos and Southern vowels,
my confessed fondness for country music.
Enviable, the ease with which the urbane

dismiss the rustic, the young dismiss
the old. So goddamn weary of being
the only one, the oddity—the queer
among the breeders, the redneck
among the silver-spoon sophisticates,

a nineteenth-century man born far
too late—day's-end I drive my dirty pickup
down kudzu back roads, wondering
what my pupils hear in that tune so often
plucked upon my Appalachian dulcimer,

> *Old times there are not forgotten*

as much the sound of home to me
as biscuits and gravy are the taste.
Burning crosses, perhaps, white hoods,
racial slurs hurled in accents like mine,
by rabid men who look like me?

> *Look away, look away*

As foul and surly as is my mood,
I pity that bourbon bottle tonight.
A Bojangles carry-out box is welcome
consolation: fried chicken breast
with attendant cole slaw, green beans,

and—yes!—a biscuit soon to be smeared
with butter and clover honey. I'm driving
the winding back road between Dublin
and Pulaski, planning a defiant mint julep
to start the evening, the truck cab fragrant

with destined dinner, the radio loud, when,
timely, as if god-sent, Brad Paisley's singing
his new hit, "Southern Comfort Zone," and
now the choir breaks into "Dixie," and I'm
grinning and humming and welling with thanks,

gray-bearded brevity rushing past golden-
rod, autumn-scruffy fields, through Virginia's eon-
gentled hills, speeding over land hundreds
of thousands of Southern soldiers died defending,
earth that breeds our years and owns our ashes

    Look away, Dixieland.

Camp Chase

2260
CONFEDERATE
    SOLDIERS
OF THE WAR 1861-1865
BURIED IN THIS
    ENCLOSURE
says the boulder, which would be only
about four hundred less than those still living
in my minuscule West Virginia hometown. Oh,
God, poor bastards, planted here like alien
seeds in stony soil, do you still dream
of escape, a regiment of yearning, bones
poised to rise on the long-awaited Judgment,
ready to march south, to Virginia and to Georgia?
You lie as tightly regulated as your dead foes
are always set, in the national cemeteries,
national meaning Yankees, *national* meaning
victors. You sleep as close as you slept
in your prisoner-of-war tent colony—starved,
freezing, passing smallpox from bed to bed—
in military rows, under neat white headstones,
an evening muster that never ends.

What I've nicknamed The Butch Store,
more widely known as Tractor Supply Company,
that's how I found you. Country boy in the big city
shopping for some solid Carhartts, chatting,
as is the Southern wont, with strangers, when
a clerk mentioned a Rebel cemetery swallowed
in the urban sprawl that is Columbus, Ohio.

Race against the sunset, as in some vampire flick,
for the place might close at dusk, but
here, now, sun's still tipping the treetops,
the gate's still open, great oaks rising
about all of you and now, briefly, me, in fallen
November, leaves like relinquished hands
the wind makes skitter and quiver, and acorns,
the pop and pop, musket fire, your hearts'
explosions waning down to this steady crunch
beneath my boots. Here's the sandstone arch,
and atop it, in perpetual vigilance, the statue of
a soldier, AMERICANS carved into the keystone
beneath his feet, as if to exhort your Northern
neighbors to show some respect. As if anyone
notices this place any longer except unreconstructed
nuts like me, or the unknown hand that's placed
by the etched boulder a tiny Stars and Bars.

Trashy tenements have replaced the erstwhile
camp, Sullivant Avenue's rush hour traffic pouring
past just over the wall, and a chubby slob
on a cell phone—furtive mutterings, suspicious
looks my way—making who knows what kind
of Sleazy-and-Scary Big-City deals. The ghostly
Lady in Gray said to walk here, mourning her fallen
love, she's nowhere to be found. I'd like to picture
some of you holding hands beneath the sod, close as
you're set, as some of you did in tents, clasping
over the narrow chasms between cots and coughs,
in the worst overcrowding two or three to a bed,

but that's too precious and too fanciful, even
for me. You died one by one, oh, God,
poor bastards, you never made it home,
the camp was torn down, sold off, modernity

rose around you decade by decade like
trash-snagging thickets of multiflora rose—
gas stations, crumbly apartments, auto
exhaust—till finally one day here I am,
striding over your bones, solemn, petty,
too late. A few minutes in the chilly sunset
before I leave you where you lie, before
I'm heading off for queer companionship at
Club Diversity, where await me popcorn, small
talk, and the biggest martinis in Columbus.

Grand Opening, Museum Of The Confederacy, Appomattox

My people, and no escaping that,
    those years I might have tried
long gone. Wild-bearded
    bikers waving a sea of Stars
and Bars, high-school vixens
    in hot pants, the sleek-suited
Richmond politicians, gingham
    country matrons, the young
firm-assed re-enactors I want
    to drag home, the diehard
plane above trailing its banner,
    Reunification by Bayonet,
which I pretty much agree with,
    even as I love nearly to the point
of eye-brine today's mélange,
    some semblance of Southern
peace that has come after
    one hundred and fifty years,
and the bloody horse-bit
    of Reconstruction
and the bitter defeat in these
    very fields that preceded that.
This Rebel soldier's buying hot dogs
    from the Black church stand,
settling down beside his blue-
    clad foe in late March sun,
comparing notes on the fine
    quality of chili and cole slaw.

Ribbon cut, the drawling crowds
      mill through the museum,
and I a part of them, past
      the sword, the uniform
Lee wore at the surrender,
      past the tattered flags
so many color-bearers
      carried defiant into death.
Only desire could tear me
      from a trance of history
so deep, and so it does,
      this boy in gray uniform,
with black bangs falling
      over his eyes, a man's
thick black beard lining
      his jaw. Brown eyes long-
lashed, shy, downcast, as if
      he were not theater but
truth, grieving a brother's
      death or the looming likelihood
of his own, he stands solemn
      beside a trio of statues,
a mother and father saying
      farewell to their son as he
prepares to leave on the eve
      of war. This little soldier's
the right age for love, I'd say,
      suppressing the usual reverent
and predatory urges I feel
      in the face of beauty: to brush
hair from his brow, squeeze
      his shoulder, pat his rear.
The right age for war, others

would opine: Sailor's Creek,
Vietnam, Iraq. He's escaped all
   of that so far, standing unbloodied
in his forebears' Rebel grey,
   black cloth bound tightly
around his right biceps.
   "Is that a mourning band?"
I ask, only pretense I can
   conceive for conversation.
"Yes, sir," he mutters, voice
   a low whisper, tight with
choked-back tears. I turn
   away for only half a minute,
false show of nonchalance,
   suppressing a useless tenderness,
and then he's vanished, never
   to be seen again, as if
he'd returned to his own time,
   the warm parlor of homecoming,
or the ditch in which he fell
   the day before the surrender.

       ◆

General Grant, I have hated you for years.
   Pit bull from Ohio, parvenu, bringing defeat
to my people, snapping turtle holding fast
   from the Wilderness to Appomattox.
But today, seeing you upon that chestnut steed,
   auburn beard framing your square jaw,
clad in the colors of a summer sky deepening
   with evening, that rich blue hue heralding
storm, well, truth be told, sir, you have never
   looked so good. Give me a hand up,
let's hear those brusque Yankee vowels,
   share a soldier's lunch of bread and bacon.

Let's talk of wrestling for position, hard-
        fought and bruise-blue compromise, victory
and the vanquished. I heartily recommend
        a one-on-one bivouac—certainly you can
trust me, sir!—in these leafing Virginia woods.

                ⬥

I suppose I should thank them,
        this chattery, obese girl with a voice
like a rutting squirrel, and her equally
        loud and corpulent boyfriend,
who babble by my side in the crowd
        sardined by the patio where occurs
today the reenactment of the surrender.
        No awed hush with these two
around, intent as they are to capture
        the moment with their precious
phone-cameras. They spare me
        tears I thought were inevitable,
watching the white-bearded and venerable
        gentleman sign the papers,
one nation's hopes end, another's begin.
        Could any of them foresee this
on that April day in 1865, the generals
        chatting amiably about mutual
acquaintances before getting down
        to immense business, the few signatures
that would end the death toll
        at six hundred and twenty thousand,
or my Rebel soldiers weeping in the meadow,
        or the enemy, silent, respectful, relieved?
Could they ever conceive that
        their descendants, the future
both sides fought for, would gather here,
        a century and a half after

all was won and all was lost, to raise,
        one by one, the flags of each Confederate
state high beside the Stars and Stripes,
        to speak their words and feign their deeds?
The acting is somewhat stiff,
        and split with awkward pauses, the mikes
only fair to middling, but there
        it is, as close to that moment as
I will ever get, but, due to the plump pair's
        indefatigable prattling,
my urge to sob is considerably
        adulterated by my urge to elbow
them both in the heads. And then
        Lee rises, he and Grant shake,
Lee leaves the imaginary parlor,
        three times pounds his left palm
with his right fist, and both generals
        mount and canter off (Grant's
skittish chestnut steed giving him some trouble).
        At last Squirrel Girl and consort
see fit to waddle off, no doubt toward
        more caloric entertainments,
and I return to spring sunlight,
        the inconsequentials of 2012,
the blooming meadows that survive us,
        the green God made to thrive on death.

Ashby Fantasia 2

Thunder in the late August distance. I'm reading
General Turner Ashby, the Centaur of the South
by Chris and Breck's pool, sprawled in board
shorts inside the cabana, sweating Richmond's
heat. *As he rides along the outposts on the white
stallion near New Market, commanding all the cavalry,
let's observe him closely since he is marked so soon
for glory and for death. Complexion, dark; height,
about five feet ten inches; weight, about
a hundred and forty-five pounds, with plume,
saber and sash.* This dusk, my boy Turner's
naked save for black Speedos, shaking water
from luxuriant whiskers in between laps
about the pool. I'm taking notes for another
poem about him, lines in sloppy pentameter,
a world in which I mix bodies and centuries
as I please, just as, come five p.m., now
I add dry vermouth to ice and gin,
a spoonful of olive juice, martinis to lure
Turner from the pool. It's necromancy of a sort,
the magic Mephistopheles used
to raise Helen of Troy from the dead and damn
Faustus forever. My hero rises from the water,
black beard down to his belly, in the constant song
of late-summer cicadas, in the scents of crepe myrtle.
Having just read how deeply he mourned his white horse,
I'm about to start the chapter describing his death
when the storm sweeps in. Turner's laughing
in the savage rain, in the high wind's trailing gauze,
his olive skin beading with wet, dark fur

thick on his thighs and trailing his belly's crest.
Maples gust-tossed now, thunder's jagged
rocks rolled across the sky. Perverse,
this passion for a long-dead man, rarely felt
for the living. Aren't legends easy to adore?
Lightning as Turner enters the cabana, as we strip
and sprawl together in the tempest, nuzzling armpits,
sipping drinks. Rain's stippling my glasses,
spotting the paper on which I compose this, control this.
Inside that insistent patter we are kissing on the couch,
twining limbs with limbs. Whimpering, Turner opens,
while hollow thunder pops like fireworks, wild rain
pocks the pool. Lightened, I lie back, licking
boy-juice from my knuckles while my dark colt dives
into shadow-waters, cuts backstrokes across
fire-streaked skies. "This is what war was,"
he says, arcing through lightning-splinter and smoke,
as if bald courage could stave off every ball and shell
and leave his heart still whole. He dives again,
does not emerge, leaving me with this pointless poem
and storm receding, rain bubbles slowing on the pool.

The Rebs In Westview Cemetery

for Donnie

So you were here, unbeknownst to me, while
I sat, cold and lonely, just down the hill,

in that shitty Harding Avenue hovel, the first of nearly
twenty years of Blacksburg rentals and deposit

checks. Here you lay, after helping to sever Stonewall's
arm, after helping Jeb Stuart drive off the Yanks,

after building back what war had broken, after
serving as presidents of Virginia Tech (dead long

before that same school banned "Dixie" at football
games). In this town I taught, I waxed passionate,

a hillbilly Heathcliff, disastrously I lost at love.
I swilled cheap beer in the Cellar, the Underground,

drank and cussed and mourned, grew grayer, plumper, met
a man with whom order and comfort could be found.

My rusty pickup here and there has skirted your ground.
Off to parties, picnics, dinners with friends,

my restlessness still quick and hot flashed past
your perfected stasis. Today, I pause

long enough to stand beside your graves, graybeard
staring into the Civil War marker's graybeard

faces, its few words teaching me some small bit
of who you were. About the axle's stillness

how wildly the wheel yet spins. Peace that complete
is a gift I hope to enter with all proper

grace only when brawnier necessities insist.
Till then, kingly Rebs, frosted gentlemen,

till our fragile fates converge where all fates must,
grass grows, early autumn's amorous quartz,

green and dewy above your bones, and here's
a blessing—a burly boy, beard as black as nuzzling

midnight—the sweet and solid some guilty god returned.
He leads me from your time-chipped tombs, back to musky

truths and sticky fur, the panting dance, hot
coffee and English breakfast at the Underground.

Laurel Hill

> Seven of the eleven children born to Archibald and Elizabeth were born here at Laurel Hill including James Ewell Brown Stuart who would, in later life, become one of the most celebrated heroes in the cause of Southern Independence.
> —www.jebstuart.org

I'm following you backwards, Beauty.
Your grave in Hollywood Cemetery,
Grace Street in Richmond where

you died, the Yellow Tavern obelisk
where you fell, and now this remote
hilltop where you spurred into the world.

It's crowded today with would-be Rebels,
Virginians like me come to celebrate
valor, commemorate suffering

and defeat, passionately devour
damned fine pulled-pork
barbeque and fry-bread tacos.

Today—despite my inversion, despite
my politely suppressed urge to abduct
one compact re-enactor with glossy

black bangs and beard—I belong
among them, the unshaven Stars-and-Bars
camo-wearing pickup-truck

crowd the groomed suburbs will never
understand. A Civil War

fashion show's first—ladies

furbelowed and preening in hoop-
skirts, with a blonde announcer, accent
as thick as mine, patiently explaining,

"Feathers is floozies. Feathers is floozies."
Nothing left of your birthplace, destroyed
by fire before the War, other than

a painting—resembling uncannily the home
of my own Confederate forebear—and a marked-
off plot adorned with marigolds,

pumpkins, and, oddly, hand-crafted
birdhouses, as if to shelter
transmigratory souls this era's

feathered. In your honor the reenactment
begins, with musket-fire, clouds
of acrid blue, sulfur's stink.

The cannons boom, the mountains resound,
great smoke-rings wafting
over the meadow till breeze tatters

their fragile fabric. Country boys
in butternut and gray slump
and fall, simulating their ancestors'

agony; the audience cheers and laughs.
Here comes the Southern cavalry,
led by your bewhiskered replica,

veering around a golden grove
of tulip trees. "Stuart will save us!"

shouts the boy in the *Praise Jesus*

T-shirt. Half a minute
after I howl, "Them Yankees ain't
playin' fair! None of 'em

are dyin'!" a stranger shouts the same.
I'm wishing our South victory, Jeb,
though there's nothing left to win.

I'm wishing I were here alone, to watch
religious light slanting down
through saber-torn clouds and silence,

to amble through pastures where no one
died and listen to October wind
rustling restively in the tulip trees,

to stand inside the very space
where a woman, straining, offered you
up to common breath, singular fate.

Yet to come, the hornet's nest,
ferocity, the suicidal
honor of the plumed cavalier.

So small, you're only pleasure, mouthfuls
of milk, a tuft of auburn hair,
eyes as blue as the day you died.

Confederate Gravestone, Charlotte Court House

Early morning in May, thick dew
on the grass, my solitude walks the cemetery

behind the Village Presbyterian Church.
Beneath huge white oaks and flowering

holly trees, I find them, my brothers,
each grave marked with a tiny replica

of the national flag
of the Confederate States of America.

On this first white stone I kneel before,
Jathro's the only letters I can make out.

Three clawed, brown-ribbed husks,
their backs ripped open, cling

to the marker's sides, and three pulsing
ruby-eyed seventeen-year cicadas.

Still moist, still mute, still stunned
with resurrection, they have risen

as predicted from the cemetery soil,
shy vanguard of the hollering hosts to come.

Notes

The quoted phrase in "Cooking for Yankees" comes from *The Life of Johnny Reb: The Common Soldier of the Confederacy* by Bell Irvin Wiley.

The italicized phrases in "Buckwheat Cakes" originally appeared in Maud Carter Clement's *War Recollections of Confederate Veterans of Pittsylvania County* and were reprinted in Patricia B. Mitchell's *Cooking for the Cause: Confederate Recipes, Documented Quotations, Commemorative Recipes*.

The italicized phrases in "Driving to Washington, D.C." come from *I Rode With Stonewall* by Henry Kyd Douglas.

Several phrases in "Snow Quilt" come from *I Rode With Stonewall* by Henry Kyd Douglas.

The italicized phrases in "Two Woodstock Menus" come from *I Rode With Stonewall* by Henry Kyd Douglas.

The italicized phrases in "Beast Butler" come from *The Story the Soldiers Wouldn't Tell: Sex in the Civil War* by Thomas P. Lowry, M.D.

The italicized section in "Ashby Fantasia 1" can be found here: http://en.wikipedia.org/wiki/Turner_Ashby

The italicized phrases in "Turner Ashby Monument, Chestnut Ridge" come from *I Rode With Stonewall* by Henry Kyd Douglas.

The italicized phrases in "Malvern Hill" come from *I Rode With Stonewall* by Henry Kyd Douglas.

The Historical Marker Database information on Moulder Hall can be found here: http://www.hmdb.org/marker.asp?marker=1947&Result=1

The italicized phrase in the third stanza of "Two Lovers at Antietam Battlefield" comes from *I Rode With Stonewall* by Henry Kyd Douglas.

The italicized phrase in "The Sweetest Music" comes from *I Rode With Stonewall* by Henry Kyd Douglas. Several details in the poem were inspired by *The History of the Rebel Yell* by Terryl W. Elliott.

The italicized phrases in "The Gallant Pelham" can be found here: http://en.wikipedia.org/wiki/John_Pelham_%28officer%29

Many of the details in "Cherry Picking" were inspired by *Four Years in the Stonewall Brigade* by John O. Casler.

The epigraph of "A Few Yards of Pickett's Charge" can be found here: http://en.wikipedia.org/wiki/George_Pickett

The italicized phrases in the third stanza of "The Fourth of July" come from *The Civil War* by Geoffrey Ward with Ric Burns and Ken Burns. The details in the fourth stanza come from *The Life of Johnny Reb: The Common Soldier of the Confederacy* by Bell Irvin Wiley.

The italicized phrase in "The Battle of New River Bridge—Radford, Virginia" can be found here: http://www.visitradford.com/Virginias_Civil_War_Trail_-_Battle_of_New_River_Bridge.aspx

The italicized phrase in "Light Rain at Saunders Field" comes from *The Dark Close Wood: The Wilderness, Ellwood and the Battle That Redefined Both* by Chris Mackowski.

Much of the information in "Lee to the Rear" comes from *The Dark Close Wood: The Wilderness, Ellwood and the Battle That Redefined Both* by Chris Mackowski. The painting referred to is included in *Don Troiani's Civil War*.

The details of the New Market Ceremony described in "Cherry Petals, VMI" can be found here: http://www.vmi.edu/vmcw/10737428744/

The epigraph and italicized phrases in "Cold Harbor" come from *The Civil War* by Geoffrey Ward with Ric Burns and Ken Burns.

The italicized phrase in "Sheridan Circle" comes from *I Rode With Stonewall* by Henry Kyd Douglas.

The quotations from Edgar Allan Poe in "The Death of Beautiful Men" are taken from his essay, "The Philosophy of Composition."

The italicized sections of "Belle Isle Prison Camp" were borrowed from *Yanks, Rebels, Rats, and Rations: Scratching for Food in Civil War Prison Camps* by Patricia B. Mitchell and two Internet sites: http://www.censusdiggins.com/prison_bellisle.html and http://www.mdgorman.com/Written_Accounts/National_Tribune/national_tribune_161887.htm

The epigraph for "Dixie" can be found here: http://en.wikipedia.org/wiki/Dixie_%28song%29 - cite_note-100

The italicized section in "Ashby Fantasia 2" comes from *General Turner Ashby, The Centaur of the South* by Clarence Thomas.

Acknowledgments

Thanks to the editors of the journals and anthologies in which some of these poems were previously published.

"The Death of Beautiful Men" — *Where Thy Dark Eye Glances: Queering Edgar Allan Poe*, edited by Steve Berman

"Confederate Kiss" — *Rebel Yell: Stories by Contemporary Southern Gay Authors*, edited by Jay Quinn

"Graves, Camp Allegheny" — *Chelsea Station*

"Fredericksburg Battlefield" — *Chelsea Station*

"Shep—December 1864" — *Chelsea Station*

"Chancellorsville" — *Poetic Voices Without Borders 2*, edited by Robert Giron

"Buckwheat Cakes" — *Now and Then: The Appalachian Magazine*

"Weeping Freak" — *Assaracus: A Journal of Gay Poetry*

"After the Reenactment 2" — *Assaracus: A Journal of Gay Poetry*

"Turner Ashby Monument" — *Assaracus: A Journal of Gay Poetry*

"Lexington Busboy" — *Assaracus: A Journal of Gay Poetry*

"A Brief Tour of McDowell, Virginia" — *Assaracus: A Journal of Gay Poetry*

"Two Woodstock Menus" — *Assaracus: A Journal of Gay Poetry*

"Two Lovers at Antietam Battlefield" — *Assaracus: A Journal of Gay Poetry*

"The Gallant Pelham" — *Assaracus: A Journal of Gay Poetry*

"A Roughed-Up Redneck" — *Assaracus: A Journal of Gay Poetry*

"In the Capitol of the Enemy" — *Assaracus: A Journal of Gay Poetry*

"The Shepherdstown Sweet Shop" — *Hard Lines: Rough South Poetry*, edited by Daniel Cross Turner and William Wright

www.ingramcontent.com/pod-product-compliance
Lightning Source LLC
Chambersburg PA
CBHW040940100426
42812CB00027B/2731/J